INPUT

OUTPUT

GETTING TO THE HEART OF PERSONAL PRAYER & BIBLE STUDY

JO BODDAM-WHETHAM

Clear and compelling, down-to-earth and practical, this is an engaging guide to getting to know God better through regular prayer and Bible reading. Full of helpful hints and teaching, I warmly commend it as a first class starter.

David Jackman

Founder of the Cornhill Training Course and past President of the Proclamation Trust

The best book to read is the Bible! The trouble is it can be hard to get into. *Input Output* is a brilliant little book that will help you get stuck into reading the Bible for yourself. Jo writes in a really easy to read, engaging way that will get you excited about the Bible and help you know how best to read it regularly. So read this book, dig deep and let it transform your Bible reading habits!

Jonathan Carswell

Managing Director

10ofThose

INPUT - OUTPUT

Getting to the Heart of Personal Prayer and Bible Study

JO BODDAM-WHETHAM

© Copyright 2013 Jo Boddam-Whetham
paperback ISBN: 978-1-78191-125-9
epub ISBN: 978-1-78191-188-4
mobi ISBN: 978-1-78191-190-7
Published by
Christian Focus Publications,
Geanies House, Fearn,
Ross-shire, IV20 1TW, U.K.
www.christianfocus.com
email:info@christianfocus.com
Cover design by Dufi-Art.com
Printed and bound by Bell and Bain

CONTENTS

INTRODUCTION

TEXTS, TWITTER, Facebook, the world wide web on your mobile phone—we can keep in touch with everyone all the time. We can find out about anything anywhere. Or can we? How do we keep in touch with the maker of the universe? How do we find out about His plans for the world? Where do I go to find out about my status before Him? No prizes for the answer. If you want to hear God speak—read the Bible! If you're eager to talk to Him—pray. You've heard that before, right? It's a Sunday school classic—if the answer isn't 'Jesus' it's probably 'read the Bible and pray'. So why do you need to use your valuable time to read a book about something so basic? Let's try a quiz!

When you get up in the morning do you:

a.   Jump out of bed, grab your Bible and prayer list and spend an hour with the Lord.

b.   Not get up at all, but go back to sleep until physically removed from the bed.

c.   Rush to get everything done that needs to get done before you leave the house.

While eating your breakfast do you:

a.   Ponder on what you have just learnt about God and pray that it will become part of your life.

b.   Not eat breakfast because you are still asleep.

c.   Check your mobile phone for messages.

When you get back in the evening do you:

a.   Put some time aside to read the Bible and pray because you didn't manage it in the morning.

b.   Turn the telly on straight away.

c.   Get down to whatever task is top on the list.

If your answers are mostly 'a's then get in touch with me and tell me where I am going wrong, because I have yet to manage it. If your answers are mainly 'b's and 'c's then read this book because like most of us you need to work on this communicating with

God thing. It's no good knowing that soap can make you clean, but never using it!

This book will not tell you how many minutes you must spend reading the Bible and praying a week. This book will not give you a magic formula that will turn Bible reading into the easiest and most inviting thing in your day.

This book will not reveal the secret time and location that are guaranteed to make Bible reading and prayer the most productive.

By God's grace though (that is with His help) this book will give you a hunger to read God's Word—the Bible—and to talk to Him regularly. It will give you some tools and advice to help you satisfy that hunger. I pray that God will use it to make time alone with God a non-negotiable that nothing else can shift.

If you have an ipod how many songs are on it? How many different opportunities to listen to music did you have today? How many text messages did you get? How many times did you update your Facebook page? What did you read? How many adverts have you seen? The floodgates are open for the messages from the world to stream into our lives—do you even open the door a centimetre to let what God has to say in? Isn't it time you did? Read on!

FOR YOUR SAFETY

Things you need to know before
you can safely read this book.

WHEN THE stewardess stands at the front of the
plane to tell you what you need to know in
the event of an emergency what do you do?
Do you listen avidly taking notes or do you
start flicking through the in-flight magazine?
To be honest we tend to turn off. Don't we?
We ignore the instructions and figure we
can sort it out on our own. And often we do!
Sometimes instructions and safety information
can be quite ridiculous!

But of course following the advice given can make the difference between life and death or at least save us a lot of time and embarrassment! Let's see how good you are at following instructions. Read through all the instructions first:

- Stand on one leg
- Sit down
- Smile
- Frown
- Laugh out loud
- Ignore instructions 1-5.

I was just testing you! Now promise you'll read the rest of this chapter before you read the rest of this book.

I pray that God will use this book to instruct and inspire you to read the Bible and pray regularly and personally. But without the following safety advice this book will be useless to you or even harmful to your health. So here we go...

SAFETY NOTE NUMBER 1

Get grace, and don't forget it!

When I started using Facebook it was all about your status. Your page opened and a little line was flashing for you to complete the sentence: Johanna Boddam-Whetham is...

I could always tell when I had been on Facebook too much when I started talking to myself in the style of a Facebook status: Johanna Boddam-Whetham is..... wondering what to do next, JB-W is..... making her bed....

At the time of printing the Facebook status is just about still there–just above 'What's on you mind'. It may be long gone by the time you read this – but humour me.

What is your (yes you reading this book!) status? Insert your name here:

_____ is: ....

Of course in one sense our 'status' changes all the time, doesn't it? We might answer the question "How are you?" several different ways over the course of a day. But what is your permanent status? Where do you stand in the scheme of the universe?

It might seem a HUGE question–but the Bible only gives us two options to choose from.

OPTION 1

Status: Made by God. In rebellion against God. Spiritually dead. Under God's judgment and facing an eternity of separation from God. What would you click on this? Like? Comment?

Their *Profile Picture* might look like this:

On their list of *Friends* you would find the world and the devil. They have no interest in sending God a *Friend request* and have denied God's request to them.

But don't take my word for it. If you're not 100% sure that this is what the Bible says, check Appendix 1 for some further reading suggestions to take you into the Bible's teaching on this in more depth.

OPTION 2

Status: Perfect in God's eyes because of His grace shown in Jesus. Alive eternally. The *Profile Picture* may look like this:

Friends: the one and only true God–Father, Son and Holy Spirit; and God's people the church.

These are two very different options. What makes the difference?

Well let's be clear what *doesn't* make the difference. The difference is *not* how many books on the Bible and prayer you have read or even how much you actually read the Bible and pray. In fact we can make no difference.

God has made the difference. We don't deserve His help. We don't deserve a change in status. It's a free undeserved gift from God.

15

That's what the Bible means by grace–the undeserved gifts that God gives us and most importantly the gift of a perfect status before Him. John 3:36 states "Whoever believes in the Son has eternal life, but whoever rejects the Son will not see life, for God's wrath[1] remains on them." Anyone who, by God's grace, believes that...

- Jesus is alive.
- Jesus is in charge of their lives and the whole world.
- Jesus died to make the difference between option 1 and 2...

has eternal life.

So, a Christian is someone who has accepted the Son–Jesus Christ. Anyone who does not accept the Son, Jesus, will remain in Option 1.

Is that the first time you have heard that you can't do anything to get sorted with God? Is it a well needed reminder that God has done everything necessary to make you His?

Or maybe you're just thinking "What a simplified version of the good news about Jesus." Well if so—you're right! An illustration using Facebook is hardly going to get across such a big truth adequately. I might as well be a toddler with finger paint trying to reproduce the Mona Lisa[2]. However if you're clear that

---

[1] anger [2] To go into more depth about what Jesus has done and what a Christian is check out the book recommendations in Appendix 1.

it is because of Jesus that God accepts us and not because of how much we read the Bible and pray then Safety Note Number 1 has done it's job. Of course there is a book that makes us completely wise about salvation, a book where we really find out about who God is, what His plans are and how He has rescued us. Got it? It's the Bible. Which means you need to keep paying attention as you read...

SAFETY NOTE NUMBER 2

Know what you're handling when
you pick up the Bible

I want to make sure we agree on some basic truths about the Bible and that we can find our way around it. Let's start by nipping a potential problem in the bud. I am getting my information about the Bible from the Bible.

I make no apology for using the Bible to find out about the Bible. The fact is that we can't find out about God on our own.

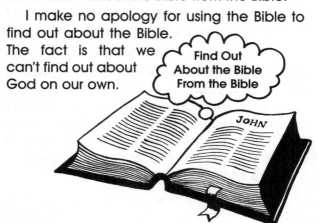

He has to show Himself to us. We often rely on people to tell us things before we can know them. For example, what might you know about me?

- When is my birthday?
- How old am I?
- How many children have I had?
- What do I eat for breakfast most days?
- What was my favourite birthday present?
- What am I thinking right now?

Now, because I live on planet earth in the twenty first century the more resourceful of you could find some of these things out. There are people you could track down and ask (don't bother, it isn't that exciting!) and of course you could use that great source of information–the internet. However, some of these questions could only be answered by me. You would only find out the answer if I revealed it to you.

Well if that is the case for me—how much more so do we need God to show Himself to us? His chosen way of doing this is through the Bible. If you're unsure about the reliability of the Bible there are some great books that show us how trustworthy the Bible is. Check them out in Appendix 1. Meanwhile, our authority is going to come from the Bible.

So what sort of book is the Bible? Is it as different from other books as we tend to think? You could, after all, pick it up, start at the beginning and read through it. It has an author—God. It starts at chapter one, page one with the creation of the universe and its final chapter ends with Jesus returning to the earth. The main character is always God (Father, Son and Holy Spirit), the main storyline is the grace God shows us in Jesus.

Have you ever thought of the Bible as one big true story? Read through my tiny summary:

- God exists for eternity.
- God makes the world perfectly.
- People sin.
- God makes promises to solve the problem of sin.
- God relates with His people Israel: sin keeps spoiling, and God keeps promising.
- God makes particular promises about sending a rescuing King to sort out sin.
- God's people wait and wait and wait and go on sinning.
- King Jesus comes. Many refuse to believe He is the King.
- The King dies on the cross—that's the rescue!
- The King rises again and ascends to heaven.
- Jesus' friends spread the news about King Jesus.

- All sorts of people become Christians– God's new people—and start meeting together.
- Lots of letters get sent to teach the new Christians all over the place.
- Jesus returns, punishes evil and makes everything new. This is the only bit that hasn't already happened–the Bible tells us to be ready for it though!
- God exists with His people, while those who are not His people exist for eternity without Him.

So the Bible is a book which tells one amazing story... But of course, there are some **major** differences between the Bible and say a novel or a magazine article we're reading. The differences lie in both its very nature – true and perfect, and in the way it is laid out.

Although it is one book, with God as its author, it is divided up into 66 different 'books', with a variety of human writers over a large passage of time.

Because we don't always read the Bible from the beginning to the end and because Bibles are all set out differently with different page numbers we need a way to all find the same bit of the Bible without starting from the beginning each time.

All the books in the Bible that describe the time before Jesus' birth make up the

Old Testament. All the books that refer to the time after Jesus was born are called the New Testament.

Each book of the Bible has a number of chapters (the bigger, bolder numbers on the page) and each chapter has a number of verses (the smaller numbers on each page).

Later on we'll be reading Paul's second letter to Timothy. It's a letter from Paul to Timothy. It's the second letter we have to Timothy in the Bible so we call it 2 Timothy, or 2nd Timothy. The bit we'll be reading is chapter 3 verses 14-17. This tends to be referred to as: 2 Tim 3:14-17. Let's try to look it up. If you have one—grab a Bible.

Start off by finding 2 Timothy. It is towards the end of the Bible. Don't worry if you have to use your contents page (you'll find that at the start of your Bible!) Just look up the page number for 2 Timothy. Then flick through until you find the large number 3. Then follow the smaller numbers to number 14. Found it? Double check using the example from the following page.

A section of the Bible like the one we have looked up is often referred to as the passage. When you hear "As we saw in this passage" it simply means the bit you have just read.

Whenever we read a passage of the Bible we need to make sure we know where we are in the flow of things. We're a bit like someone

2 Timothy

(3) But mark this: There will be terrible times in the last days. ² People will be lovers of themselves, lovers of money, boastful, proud, abusive, disobedient to their parents, ungrateful, unholy, ③ without love, unforgiving, slanderous, without self-control, brutal, not lovers of the good, ④treacherous, rash, conceited, lovers of pleasure rather than lovers of God— ⁵ having a form of godliness but denying its power. Have nothing to do with them.

> This number 3 is referring to chapter 3 of 2 Timothy

> These smaller numbers are referring to the different verses within chapter 3.

> The highlighted section is 2 Timothy chapter 3 verses 14-17.

⁶They are the kind who worm their way into homes and gain control over weak-willed women, who are loaded down with sins and are swayed by all kinds of evil desires, ⁷always learning but never able to acknowledge the truth. ⁸Just as Jannes and Jambres opposed Moses, so also these men oppose the truth—men of depraved minds, who, as far as the faith is concerned, are rejected. ⁹But they will not get very far because, as in the case of those men, their folly will be clear to everyone.

¹⁰You, however, know all about my teaching, my way of life, my purpose, faith, patience, love, endurance, ¹¹persecutions, sufferings— what kinds of things happened to me in Antioch, Iconium and Lystra, the persecutions I endured. Yet the Lord rescued me from all of them. ¹²In fact, everyone who wants to live a godly life in Christ Jesus will be persecuted, ¹³while evil men and impostors will go from bad to worse, deceiving and being deceived. *¹⁴But as for you, continue in what you have learned and have become convinced of, because you know those from whom you learned it, ¹⁵and how from infancy you have known the holy Scriptures, which are able to make you wise for salvation through faith in Christ Jesus. ¹⁶All Scripture is God-breathed and is useful for teaching, rebuking, correcting and training in righteousness, ¹⁷so that the man of God may be thoroughly equipped for every good work.*

parachuting out of a plane into the middle of nowhere—we'll want to take a look at a map first.

So each time we take a look at a passage we'll stop and find out where we are in the Bible. I've called this ORIENTATION. We'll look at how to do this when we get to chapter 8, up to that point I've done the hard work for you. You just have to read it.

A final warning about picking up the Bible.

The Bible describes itself as a very sharp double edged sword (Hebrews 4:12[3]). This means that the Bible can pierce our soul; get right into our lives; look right into us; and judge us accordingly.

Have you read 'The Lion, The Witch and the Wardrobe?' by C.S. Lewis? When the four children find out that they are going to meet a lion (Aslan) they are rightly a bit wary. They ask nervously "Is he—quite safe?". The answer they get is excellent. "'Course he isn't safe. But he's good"[4]. The Bible is not a safe book, but it is a good book. Which brings me to...

---

[3] For the ORIENTATION and a longer look at this verse see chapter 5, page 82.

[4] Taken from *The Lion, The Witch and The Wardrobe*, by C.S. Lewis; page 75 of the 1996 edition published by Diamond Books, a division of HarperCollins Publishers

SAFETY NOTE NUMBER 3

I'm not going to do all the talking

Be prepared to pray

Let's pray for God's help before we read the Bible and then thank Him for what we have read and discovered. Let's ask for God's help as we respond to the amazing truths we find out about Him and the disgusting ones we find out about ourselves.

Remember—it's God's work to sort out our status before Him. Grace. It's God's work to enable us to pick up and handle His Word. Grace. It's God's work to help us do something with what we read. Grace. By God's grace it is our privilege to get involved not only in God's work in our lives, but in His work throughout the world!

If you've really got Safety Note Numbers 1 and 2 you are going to want to talk to God. You may be the most confident person you know when it comes to explaining what our status is before God with and without Jesus. You may be able to explain God's grace miles better than me. You may be the quickest in class to look up any Bible reference. BUT if you are not talking to God it won't mean much. For now don't worry about the how and why of prayer–we'll get to that. Just be prepared to start talking to God. So have you read...

SAFETY NOTE NUMBER 1

Get grace, and don't forget it!

It's because of Jesus that God accepts us not because of how much we read the Bible and pray!

YES..... NO.....I SKIPPED IT.....

And...

SAFETY NOTE NUMBER 2

Know what you're handling when you pick up the Bible

The Bible is our authority on these matters, it is by God, it is completely true and perfect, and each bit needs to be read as part of a whole.

YES..... NO ..... I SKIPPED IT.....

And finally...

SAFETY NOTE NUMBER 3

I'm not going to do all the talking
Be prepared to pray
YES..... NO..... I SKIPPED IT.....

Time Out: Let's pray now. Thank God for His grace, thank God for the Bible and thank God that we can talk to Him and ask for His help.

And we're back...

If you answered yes for all three you may proceed! If you haven't—don't blame me when the plane crashes! You've been given the safety instructions! You need to pay attention!

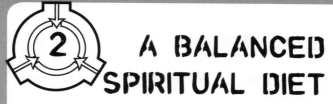

2 A BALANCED SPIRITUAL DIET

The place prayer and Bible reading can have in
our everyday lives

WELL DONE–you've got this far. Have you gathered that I want you (Yes, YOU–not your parents, your youth leader or your big brother[1]) to read the Bible and pray?

Maybe this is a totally new concept for you–if so, great! Keep reading. By the end of this book Bible reading and prayer should be something you not only want to do, but also feel able to make a start at. (If I've done my job properly that is!)

Or just maybe you are struggling not to yawn at this stage. Maybe you are considering putting the book down. "I do read the Bible and pray!—you protest. "I've been doing that since before I can remember! I go to a church where they read the Bible every Sunday, we study it at youth group, we even occasionally read it at school if that counts! And prayer—of course—church, youth group, at home before meals. Are you saying that's not enough?"

---

[1] Please note I do want these people to read the Bible—but right now I'm talking to YOU!

The short answer, the answer the Bible gives us, is *"No it is not enough!"*

Have a look at the passage below. But... PAUSE! Find out what you're reading—get orientated.

ORIENTATION FOR PSALM 119

Which book of the Bible is this passage from? Psalms. This is a collection of poetry and songs. Different people wrote the Psalms – sometimes the Bible tells us who they were and when they wrote and sometimes it doesn't. Some psalms were said or sung when God's people gathered together. Christians still do this when they gather together today.

You will find the book of Psalms right in the middle of your Bible. It is in the Old Testament. It was written before Jesus was born. Lots of psalms refer to the time of King David, in fact many were written by him, about him and for him. But psalms were written and sung long after King David too.

WHAT ELSE SHOULD I KNOW?

- When you read these verses you won't find the word <u>Bible</u> used. In fact the writer of Psalm 119 uses six different phrases to refer to what God says (that's poetry for you—it adds emphasis and richness!) I've underlined them for you.

- The Psalmist (the person who wrote the psalm) didn't have the whole Bible as we do. He just had the first five books. However, we can apply what the writer says to the whole Bible.

- The writer is talking to God so the 'you' in the passage is The LORD God.

PLAY: PSALM 119:9-16

⁹ How can a young person stay on the path of purity?
By living according to your <u>Word</u>.
¹⁰ I seek you with all my heart;
do not let me stray from your <u>commands</u>.
¹¹ I have hidden your Word in my heart
that I might not sin against you.
¹² Praise be to you, LORD;
teach me your <u>decrees</u>.
¹³ With my lips I recount
all the <u>laws</u> that come from your mouth.
¹⁴ I rejoice in following your <u>statutes</u>
as one rejoices in great riches.
¹⁵ I meditate on your <u>precepts</u>
and consider your ways.
¹⁶ I delight in your decrees;
I will not neglect your word.

Look at the action words. What does the writer want to do? What doesn't he want to do?

Don't worry about every detail of the Psalm – read it through again and get a feel for what the writer is saying and why he is saying it.

Now think about this. Would the writer of this Psalm be satisfied with reading God's words once or twice a week? Would he mind missing a week because something else came up? Do you think he only reads it when there is a Bible study on that he can go to?

- Sure!
- Maybe.
- No way!

If you said "No way" then I'm with you.

It's excellent to hear the Bible read and taught at church and youth group. It's great to pray with other people. Don't stop! But that only meets part of your needs. Think about our physical bodies. You need a balanced diet of all the different food groups, you need exercise and sleep….well let's say that if time with others reading the Bible and praying is one part of a healthy spiritual diet then reading and praying alone is another vital element.

Let's look at another Psalm. Our ORIENTATION is the same as our last passage so we can dive right in.

PLAY: PSALM 1:1-3.

Go on – look it up. Hint: Psalms are usually about half way through your Bible. Just in case you're reading this on the bus and you haven't got your Bible with you here it is:

¹ Blessed is the one
    who does not walk in step with the wicked
or stand in the way that sinners take
    or sit in the company of mockers,
² but whose delight is in the law of the LORD,
    and who meditates on his law day and night.
³ That person is like a tree planted by streams of water,
    which yields its fruit in season
and whose leaf does not wither—
    whatever they do prospers.

Read verse 1, and compare it to verse 2 and verse 3. Did you spot the two contrasting pictures here? There are two potential sources of authority, guidance and influence described. Verse 1 tells us where **not** to get our input from, while verses 2 and 3 give us an inviting picture of a life soaked in God's Word.

31

The first picture is of someone getting very stuck. His companions are the wicked, the sinners, those who mock God. Can you see this man grinding to a halt? He starts walking beside them, but by the end of the verse he is sitting down comfortably with completely the wrong set of influences. He's not going anywhere in a hurry! Nor is the tree in verses 2 and 3! It isn't dipping into the stream once a week. The stream is its constant source of nourishment and refreshment. The man who is sorted is the man who meditates on God's Word day and night.

Never mind the details of what that might actually look like – for now just get a sense of the writer's attitude to God's Word. Would he be happy with a week spent walking, standing and sitting with those who are against[1] God as long as he got a 'good drink' of God's Word on a Sunday morning? I don't think so.

Let's pause and consider our lives. Be honest – it's for your eyes only – oh and God's – but He already knows! In and around the picture of the chair scribble down various chances you give yourself to...

- Receive the advice of people who don't love Jesus.

- Hear and see the input of non-Christians.

---

[1]Which includes those apparently disinterested and totally ignoring God as well as those openly against God.

- Get involved in the ways of people who don't accept the rule of Jesus.

- Adopt or tolerate a scoffing attitude towards God.

Check yourself in your thinking, your behaving, and your belonging. What would a fly on the wall documentary say about how at ease you are in that comfy chair? What if it recorded all that you have listened to, watched, involved yourself in, talked about...?

Now look at the tree drawing below. Jot down in and around it the opportunities you give yourself to receive and consider the Word of God. On a scale of 1-10 how rooted are you by that stream?

1 (not rooted _____

_____10 (very rooted)

How are you feeling? Excited? Guilty? Ready to shut the book and give up? Please don't give up. Remember Safety Note Number 1 in the previous chapter!

How often we spend reading the Bible doesn't change what God thinks of us. If we have accepted what Jesus has done for us we are completely forgiven, completely accepted and completely loved. Reading the Bible more won't make God love you more, reading it less won't make God love you less.

What these Psalms are teaching us is that our love for Jesus should make the Bible an ever greater part of our lives. One of the best things we can do, with God's help, is to develop a pattern of regular Bible reading. As we read and digest these Psalms our thinking should change from "Why should I read the Bible more?" to "Why wouldn't I? When can I start?"

So basically the Bible is unashamedly biased. "Read me—read me a lot!" We've seen it in the Psalms, but there are loads of passages that give the same impression. Let's look at something from the New Testament—Colossians 3:16. No don't! PAUSE! and find out what you're reading.

ORIENTATION: COLOSSIANS

Where is Colossians in the Bible? In the New Testament, after the four Gospels. The Gospels tell us about Jesus' life, death and resurrection. As we read the rest of the New Testament (for example Colossians) we need to remember that Jesus has risen again and returned to Heaven. The news about Him is spreading and His people are waiting for His return.

WHAT ELSE SHOULD I KNOW?

This book is a letter from a Christian called Paul to Christians living in a place called Colossae. Take a look at chapter 1:1–2 if you want to check.

Other teachers tried to get the Colossian Christians to do extra things to make God pleased with them. Paul told them to stick with Jesus and keep focused on Him. OK—now you can read it. Don't miss it, it's a short one.

PLAY: COLOSSIANS 3:16

"Let the Word of Christ dwell in you richly...."

Yes, that's it! Go on read it again. You could even memorise this one.

Which phrase best describes the place that Paul wants the Bible to have in our lives?

- A quick visit at Christmas.
- Moved in permanently.

• Regularly pops in for the weekend.

Which word in the passage tells us this? That's right—the Word of Christ is meant to *dwell* in us. To dwell in us richly. When it comes to Bible reading we shouldn't be economical and stingy. Nor are we counting calories. Our reading of the Bible should be a rich feast not a celery stick and a cracker.

So—from what we've read in God's Word so far—can we truthfully say that reading the Bible on your own is a God pleasing, advisable habit to form? Definitely! It won't be easy so we need to know this!

Now it's time to get a taste for what the Bible teaches us about praying regularly by ourselves. Read the following verses and tell me what flavour you're picking up.

ORIENTATION

The first two passages are from the Gospels. The accounts written down about Jesus' time on this earth, right at the start of the New Testament. The first is a man called Mark telling us something about Jesus and the second is Jesus teaching His disciples (those who followed and learned from Jesus).

PLAY: MARK 1 :35

Very early in the morning, while it was still dark, Jesus got up, left the house and went off to a solitary place, where he prayed.

PLAY MATTHEW 6 :9-13

"This, then, is how you should pray:

'Our Father in heaven, hallowed be your name, your kingdom come,your will be done, on earth as it is in heaven.

Give us today our daily bread.
And forgive us our debts,as we also have forgiven our debtors.
And lead us not into temptation,but deliver us from the evil one.'

ORIENTATION

The following passages are all in the New Testament and are all from letters written by Paul to various churches.

PLAY: EPHESIANS 1:15-17

For this reason, ever since I heard about your faith in the Lord Jesus and your love for all God's people, I have not stopped giving thanks for you, remembering you in my prayers. I keep asking that the God of our Lord Jesus Christ, the glorious Father, may give you the Spirit of wisdom and revelation, so that you may know Him better.

PHILIPPIANS 1:3-4

I thank my God every time I remember you. In all my prayers for all of you, I always pray with joy.

PLAY: PHILIPPIANS 4:4-6

Rejoice in the Lord always. I will say it again: Rejoice! Let your gentleness be evident to all. The Lord is near. Do not be anxious about anything, but in every situation, by prayer and petition, with thanksgiving, present your requests to God.

PLAY: COLOSSIANS 1:3

We always thank God, the Father of our Lord Jesus Christ, when we pray for you.

PLAY: 1 THESSALONIANS 1:2

We always thank God for all of you and continually mention you in our prayers.

What is the main flavour coming through? I'm getting a strong taste of regular prayer, both planned and spontaneous. Let's follow the example that Jesus Himself gave us. Let's ask our Heavenly Father for daily provision as Jesus instructed. If Paul wants us to talk to God as often as we are tempted to worry, and to thank Him continually then prayer has got to be a significant part of our lives. If Paul was praying so passionately for all the churches and people he was writing to then the sheer volume of prayer points must have made regular, organised prayer necessary!

So if we are letting the Bible set our agenda then regular, individual prayer and Bible study will be non-negotiable. Here's a list of things that some young people said happened in their every day lives:

- brush my teeth
- wake up
- sleep
- eat
- computer games
- ipod/music
- shower/bath
- school
- laptop stolen by sister
- Sunday lunch
- homework
- relax
- swimming
- read
- time with friends
- tv
- family time
- look after pets
- play games
- argue with sister
- text
- smile and laugh
- go to the loo
- get dressed
- jump and shout
- exercise
- dance

- play violin
- breathe

Everyone's list will be different. Although there are some there which we will all do everyday! What is it that you can't imagine a day without doing?

One of mine would be using my face-wash before I go to sleep! If I'm tucked up and I realise I haven't done this daily ritual, the fear of a bad complexion will get me out of my bed to do it. And yet–why is it that I'll go to sleep and leave time with God to tomorrow, night after night?

Well we'll consider some of the reasons and how to do battle with them later on. For now we've recognised the love of God's Word and the heart for prayer that the Bible holds out to us to grab hold of. I hope you're tempted by the taster. If so you'll want to get a bit more practical. What is it we are actually talking about doing day to day? See you in the next chapter.

IT'S QUIET TIME

How to start regular prayer
and Bible reading

SO HOW do we make reading the Bible and praying part of our lives? We're talking about this because the Bible makes it clear that God's Word to us and our prayers to Him need to be a big part of our day!

WHAT'S IN A NAME?

Have you ever heard anyone talk about having a quiet time? Maybe a Christian youth leader has mentioned something they learnt in their quiet time that morning, or your Mum or Dad might ask not to be interrupted while they have one. Maybe someone has asked you about your quiet times and you're thinking: "What are you talking about?"

Of course there are all sorts of different names people use for basically the same thing. Perhaps you've heard it called a daily devotional or Bible time....well it doesn't really matter what you call it. You won't find any of these phrases in the Bible. But having a name for what we're talking about will make my job simpler. It just takes too long to type out 'regular, individual prayer and Bible study'! We could call it Fred, but I think there's some value in the phrase Quiet Time.

This is what I'm talking about when I talk about a quiet time: a specific, planned slot of time in which you can be quiet in order to...

- read a specific passage from the Bible.
- think about it.
- pray about it.
- pray for your day.
- pray for a variety of people and situations.

So it's quiet (think undisturbed and focused, rather than sedate and silent) and it's a time. While there is never a time when you shouldn't pray and read the Bible, it's important that there are slots of time specifically given over to those tasks.

DOES IT HAVE TO BE ALONE?

While it is absolutely vital to hear the Bible taught by skilled Bible teachers it is also important to handle God's Word yourself. We never grow out of being fed by preaching and teaching, but we need to grow into reading the Bible for ourselves. Perhaps you have a regular slot for praying and reading the Bible, but you do it with a parent, a sibling or a friend. Fantastic! My daughter is six and we really enjoy doing this together. Gradually though the time will come for her to have a go on her own. The first step might be reading the Bible on her own but with me there. This way the habit is less likely to slip, help is at hand and we can maybe pray and chat about what she has read when she has finished.

So let's get practical. Here you are. You have heard about what God has done for sinners through Jesus and you want to put Him in charge of your life – or at least explore what it would mean to do so. You've read the previous chapters and you are convinced that having a quiet time needs to be a priority in your day. Not because I say so – but because God does. So what do you do? You could:

a. start by asking God to help you form a life long habit or

b. pick up the Bible and start

While we need to avoid constantly putting the whole thing off, we do need to recognise that this is going to be a battle. As sinners you and I will always tend towards pushing God and His Word out of our lives and the world we live in will cheer us along! So the best start we can make is by praying.

Some of you will hate the idea of routine and sticking to a habit. You need to pray for God's help. Others of you may feel quietly confident in your ability to be planned and disciplined. You need to pray too. Sheer willpower may keep you going through the motions for a while, but only God can make you be like that tree flourishing by the stream in Psalm 1.

Every time we manage to have a quiet time we should thank God and ask for Him to help us again tomorrow. Every time we fail we need to say sorry and ask for God's help to get going again. Every Christian I know (and I'm married to a vicar!) slips up in this area and needs to go on pleading with God for His help.

So if step 1 is—pray for help, what should you do next?

a. wait for God to wake you up early one morning just feeling like reading your Bible and praying.

b. make some specific, realistic, and appropriate plans for a quiet time.

Think back to the list of things you do everyday. A few will happen naturally – breathing and arguing for example! However, most happen because someone has planned for it to happen. I guess for you lots of things happen because other people have planned well – you have a clean school uniform, there is food in the fridge or a meal ready at the right time. But increasingly there will be things that will only happen if you make them happen.

• A certain top you want to take on holiday will only get through the wash in time if you think ahead and put it in the washing basket.

- Planning your own work schedule so that things get handed in on time.
- Setting 'series record' for your favourite programme before you go away for a few days.

If we want something to happen (either because we love it and/or because we know it is important) we will plan for it. The more unimportant something is to us and/or the more unappealing something is—the less likely we are to make it happen.

For me, going to the gym is really important. Even when I don't feel like going! So I plan really carefully to make it happen. When my baby was tiny a friend looked after him for an hour in the morning so that I could go, now I get up horribly early so that I can get back in time to take my children to school. This in turn means I need to make the packed lunches the night before and get to bed early. Sorry to bore you with my domestic details—but hopefully you get the idea. The challenge for me is—do I make the same effort to have a quiet time—and if not—why not?

So our plans for having a quiet time need to be specific, realistic and appropriate.

Consider the following:

1. When will you do it?
2. Where will you do it?
3. How long can you realistically plan to spend on it?

Then consider which of these factors will vary through the week. Read through the ideas below and spot the vague, unrealistic and inappropriate answers given to the questions above. What is wrong with the plans these people are making? Which traps have you or are you likely to fall into yourself?

- "I'll have a quiet time twice a day for an hour–I'm not sure what I'll stop doing to make the time, but I'll squeeze it in somewhere."

- "On Tuesday I'll read the Bible at 6.47am, then pray at 7.09pm. On a Wednesday I'll try 8pm, except on the third Wednesday in the month when I'll change to 4.08pm to fit in with film club."

- "I'll just see how each day goes–it will happen."

- "I've normally got 3 minutes if I have my shower before my sister–unless I'm washing my hair–I'll fit it in there."

- "I'll have breakfast in my room and do my quiet time there. Mum thinks it's important family time and needs my help with the younger kids. Some days it is the only time I see Dad, but tough."

- "I will wake up three hours earlier every morning."
- "I'll have my quiet time just before I go to sleep–I normally can't keep my eyes open, but I'm sure I'll manage if I prop myself up on my pillow a bit. I could do it at my desk to help me stay awake– but that would be too cold!"
- "I'll use the time I have on the school bus–it's a bit bumpy and noisy, and I'll have to cover up what I'm doing to avoid comments, but it will do."

The positive thing is that most of these people are at least trying to make a plan! The problem is the plans are not all that appropriate and will either never happen, quickly die out or just won't produce a very helpful time praying and reading the Bible.

Of course there are lots of things we will have to juggle and tricky things we'll really struggle with. We'll come back to this later on with some practical pointers. We'll also put our specific, realistic and appropriate planning into practice as we consider how to use this brilliantly planned time! Most importantly we'll consider together what to do when days go by and we haven't opened our Bible or uttered a prayer and we'll remember that Jesus has got it covered. For now: We have prayed for God's help to have a quiet time We have planned to make it happen

WHAT NEXT?

Which of the following steps would you advise?

1. Get on with it and make a start.
2. Put it off until after exams or holidays.
3. Wait until you know a bit more about it.
4. Tell no one so no one will know if you struggle.
5. Tell everyone so they will know how brilliant you are.
6. Encourage a friend to make a start with you so you can help each other.
7. Give an older Christian permission to check up on you.
8. Keep reading this book to find out more (I'll be upset if you don't tick this one!).
9. Be pleased that finally you can be sure that you will go to heaven now you are having a quiet time.
10. Get grace, keep it in mind and don't forget it. Remember Safety Note Number 1 – go on read it again!

I'm sure you've ticked all the right ones – but to set my mind at rest I would advise the following: 1, 6, 7, 8!, and 10.

Before we go any further I want you to meet three friends of mine and find out a bit about their quiet times.

INTERVIEWS

Firstly meet Trudi who's nearly 18.

Hi, what's your name?

Trudi

Have you ever had a quiet time?

Yes

When and how were you introduced to quiet times?

Aged 11 at a Pathfinder camp. Our dorm looked at the Bible together each morning as a group and we were encouraged to continue it alone when we got home using some Bible reading notes we were given.

Do you currently have a quiet time?

Yes. I use something which comes to my mobile as a daily e-mail.

Where do you have it?

In the lounge.

When do you have it?

While having breakfast.

How long is it?

5-10 minutes

Has your quiet time always been like that?

No.

If not what changed?

The material I was using.

Have you ever gone a long time without having a quiet time? If so what happened?

Yes. I got out of the habit of doing it. The notes I used got neglected. They never seemed to be in the right place and if I missed it first thing I couldn't catch up during the day because my notes were somewhere else!

How did you start again?

My dad encouraged me to try again using different notes. It is much harder to avoid an e-mail that comes to my phone and it goes with me during the day. Dad uses the same system so that we can chat about what we have read. The first quiet time after the long gap was about God's grace which was perfect!

Next up is Nikki aged...mid 20s....

Hi, what's your name? ——— Nikki

Have you ever had a quiet time? — Yes

How were you introduced to quiet times?

It was a year after I became a Christian, so about 8 years ago. I was meeting a friend to read the Bible each week and she told me that she had something called a 'quiet time'. I asked what it was and how to do it and it started from there.

Do you currently have a quiet time?

Yes. I have it on the sofa. First thing in the morning.

How long is it?

20 mins to half an hour, longer at the weekends.

Has your quiet time always been like that?

No. I try and vary it because otherwise I can get stuck in a rut. A wise friend told me it was OK to do different things in your quiet time.

How has it changed?

It has been longer, shorter, at different times of day and in different places.

Have you ever gone a long time without having a quiet time?

No

Any practical pointers to help us?

I just keep doing it—even if I don't feel like it or I can only squeeze in 5-10 minutes. I try and do it at my best time of day (when I concentrate best) —for me, the morning. Sometimes I just read a bit of the Bible and think about it, sometimes I use notes, I pray in different ways such as out loud, singing, or writing prayers down.

And finally meet Tom.

Hi, what's your name?

> I'm Tom. I live in Sevenoaks, Kent and I'm thirteen.

Do you currently have a quiet time?

> Yes, I still read the Bible with my Dad in the evenings, but I also do a Bible study, which I receive everyday on my ipod.

Where do you have it?

> I read the Bible with my Dad in my bedroom and I do my ipod study at the breakfast table, or sometimes in my bedroom.

When do you have it?

> I read the Bible with my Dad in the evenings at our family prayer time. I do my ipod study at breakfast (normally around 7:10) or sometimes before 7 if I wake up early.

How long is it?

> Normally about 10-15 mins with my Dad and 5-10 mins by myself.

Has your quiet time always been like that?

No. I didn't always read the Bible on my ipod.

If not—what made it change?

I suppose I wanted to read some stuff on my own. I won't always have my Dad to read with me!

Have you ever gone a long time without having a quiet time?

Sometimes I miss a few days. I forget to do the Bible reading on my ipod as I am forgetful and one of those people who says, "Oh yeah, I'll do that later" and then "Not now, I'll do it tomorrow" etc. Also other things distracted me like reading the news.

How did you start again?

I made it part of my routine again, so that it was the first thing that I did when I came downstairs for breakfast.

So that's what some of my friends do. What about you? What can you take from this chapter to help you get started?

Apparently it takes 5 weeks to form a habit. In other words if we do something regularly for 5 weeks it might just have a chance to get rooted into the fabric of our lives. (It also means that we can't really say something hasn't worked until we've tried it for a good few weeks!) Are you up for that? Remember you have your whole life to keep it going and unlimited chances to start again when you don't.

QUICK QUESTION: TRUE OR FALSE?

If I read the Bible and pray everyday for one hour, if I read through the whole Bible every year and pray for at least 10 people – including missionaries I will go to heaven.

To discover the answer look back to Safety Note Number 1 and keep reading.

4 WRIGGLING OUT OR DIVING IN!

Why it is worth taking the plunge

BY THE way the answer to the last question is false! So let's keep reading. When you get up in the morning what is it you really look forward to? Which parts of your week do you dive into willingly and which make you squirm like a worm on a hook? What do you do your best to wriggle out of?

When it comes to reading the Bible we tend to ask (or at least think) "Are you sure I have to? Does it really say that?"

Our next question might be: "What is the shortest time I can spend and it still count? Could I do it every other day instead? Can I take Saturdays off?"

If we are honest, when it comes to Bible reading we try to wriggle out rather than dive in! Basically, we're worms rather than deep sea divers!

In fact, I have just had to stop typing because I realised that I hadn't spent time reading God's Word today! Here I was writing a book about it and I hadn't actually done it. Wriggle, wriggle! There that's better!

As I write this book and you read it we should be asking ourselves: Why don't I spend more time in personal prayer and Bible reading? Why hasn't any one told me about this before? Why didn't I listen when they did?

By God's grace (that means it needs to be Him working in us as we can't change our thinking on our own!), a light will switch on in our thinking and in our hearts that will help us develop a lifelong habit.

Remember the Psalms we read in chapter 2? Could we also have that love of God's Word?

WHAT ARE WE DOING WHEN
WE READ THE BIBLE?

Have you ever heard the expression: "It does what it says on the tin"? It means that the label tells you simply and clearly what's inside and you'll find exactly that when you take a look.

I want to study a brilliant part of the Bible with you. If the Bible was a tin we could put this on the label! These verses will help us see what the Bible is and why we should dive deeply and regularly into reading it. So get your Bible out. Don't wriggle away. But don't dive straight in! PAUSE!

Remember the parachutist who took a good look at the map before jumping out of the plane? Let's make sure we know where we are in the flow of things so that we can properly understand the verses we are about to read.

ORIENTATION: 2 TIMOTHY

Where is 2 Timothy in the Bible? The New Testament, after the Gospels. Jesus has come to earth as a baby, has died and risen again and returned to Heaven. His people are waiting for His return.

WHAT ELSE SHOULD I KNOW?

2 Timothy is a letter (2 Timothy 1:1-2). It was written by the apostle Paul to his friend Timothy; a young man who had worked alongside Paul. When Paul wrote this letter Timothy was teaching and helping some churches in a place called Ephesus.

- Why is Paul writing? Paul is about to be killed for loving Jesus. He wants Timothy to keep his work going. It is a training letter for Timothy so that he can be a great church leader. Paul knows this is probably his last contact with Timothy so we see here what is most important to Paul and why. (1:13, 2:2, 4:6)

- What has Paul already told Timothy in this letter? Paul wants Timothy to keep the truth about Jesus safe. He mustn't change it, add anything, take away the bits he doesn't like....but he can't just bury it away. He can't lock it in a vault – he has to pass it on to other people who will also keep it safe.

  Paul has also told Timothy that this isn't going to be easy. There was (as there still is today) strong opposition to the truth about Jesus. Remember—Paul is about to die for doing the job he is handing over to Timothy.

So ORIENTATION over—let's take a quick breather with a true or false quiz.

TRUE OR FALSE?

1. The part of the body most sensitive to pain is the brain.

2. 90% of all Earth's life forms are now extinct.

3. Ancient Chinese hunters used tame lions instead of hunting dogs.

4. The first handkerchiefs were used by ancient Greeks. They considered giving the nose a loud blow to be refined.

5. After hearing his cat running on the piano keys, Chopin composed a cat waltz.

6. If a chameleon is put on a chequered surface, it will become chequered itself within 20 minutes.

7. Hot dogs were sold at Roman amphitheatres.

8. Some dinosaurs had eight hearts.

9. Hamsters sleep with their eyes open.

10. The swan lies on its back in the water when it wants to wash the feathers on its back.

Check your answers at the bottom of the next page. How did you do?

For the next questions only you know the answers! Answer true or false for the following statements about you.

1. I would rather find out the truth about something even if it is hard to hear.
2. I would prefer to go on believing something that was untrue, but comfortable.
3. I would rather tell people the truth on all occasions.
4. I prefer to tell people what they want to hear even when it is untrue.

Answered those? Good. Now where were we? We've looked before leaping and have an idea of what we are jumping into: A letter from Paul to Timothy in which Paul gives Timothy the job of sticking with the truth about Jesus and passing it on despite the prevailing culture of lies. We've had a quick breather–now we dive in!

Answers: 1. False – the brain can't feel anything. It is possible to perform surgery on it without the patient feeling any pain at all. 2. True. 3. True. 4. False. 5. True – he tried to reproduce the cat's walk over the keys. 6. False. 7. True. 8. True – several hearts were necessary to pump blood through their huge bodies. 9. False. 10. True. Information taken from 'True or False' produced by MB Games, copyright 1995 Hasbro International Inc.

PLAY! READ 2 TIMOTHY 4:1-5

Please note the words in italics are to help you pick up on Paul's different ways of talking about the truth about Jesus.

[1]In the presence of God and of Christ Jesus, who will judge the living and the dead, and in view of His appearing and His kingdom, I give you this charge: [2]Preach the *Word*; be prepared in season and out of season; correct, rebuke and encourage—with great patience and careful instruction. [3]For the time will come when people will not put up with *sound doctrine*. Instead, to suit their own desires, they will gather around them a great number of teachers to say what their itching ears want to hear. [4]They will turn their ears away from the *truth* and turn aside to myths. [5]But you, keep your head in all situations, endure hardship, do the work of an evangelist, discharge all the duties of your ministry.

Did you spot how popular the truth was in Timothy's day? On a scale of 1—10: about a zero. I don't know how you answered the four personal true and false questions on the previous page, but in Timothy's situation lies were much more popular than the truth.

Read 2 Timothy chapter 4 verses 3 and 4 again. Fill in the gaps using these words: away; teachers; hear, myths; truth.

The time is coming when people will not put up with the _____. They will gather around them _____ to tell them what they want to _____. They will turn their ears _____ from the truth and listen to _____ instead.

Throughout the letter Paul urges Timothy to be different from those who hunger for lies and from those who spread them.

- Not because the truth was the easy option–it wasn't.

- Not because the truth was the safest option–it wasn't.

- Not because it was the popular option–it wasn't.

But because the truth was the best option.

Read Paul's description of the truth and truth tellers.

PLAY: READ 2 TIMOTHY 3:10-17

[10]You, however, know all about my teaching, my way of life, my purpose, faith, patience, love, endurance, [11]persecutions, sufferings—what kinds of things happened to me in Antioch, Iconium and Lystra, the persecutions I endured. Yet the Lord rescued me from all of them. [12]In fact, everyone who wants to live a godly life in Christ Jesus will be persecuted, [13]while evildoers and impostors will go from bad to worse, deceiving and being deceived. [14]But as for you, continue in what you have learned and have become convinced of,

because you know those from whom you learned it, [15]and how from infancy you have known the Holy Scriptures, which are able to make you wise for salvation through faith in Christ Jesus. [16]All Scripture is God-breathed and is useful for teaching, rebuking, correcting and training in righteousness, [17]so that the servant of God may be thoroughly equipped for every good work.

Did you spot anything Paul told Timothy that will encourage you to dive into the truth of God's Word daily? Underline anything that struck you about God's Word. Imagine Paul was writing an advert for the truth. Here are some 'selling points' that I found.

SELLING POINT 1

People who pass on the truth, live by the truth (2 Timothy 3:14); and will be prepared to suffer for it. Timothy knew Paul well (2 Timothy 3:10). Paul knew Timothy's grandmother and his mum (2 Timothy 1:5).

There's all sorts of rubbish we can listen to, but if you really want to test a message —get to know the person telling it. The truth tellers in Timothy's life lived a life consistent with what they taught. Not everyone who tells you about Jesus will live a perfect life (none of them will!). However, their lives will fit with the truth they are speaking. If there isn't a match—be careful about listening to them.

SELLING POINT 2

The truth will make you wise for salvation (2 Tim 3:15). Paul tells Timothy that the truth will help save him. Does that strike you as odd? Paul has already told Timothy very clearly that if he speaks the truth and lives by it he will face trouble. Now he says it's the truth that will rescue him! So which is true? Does the truth put you in the way of danger and trouble or rescue you from it? Well they are both true. It all depends what sort of trouble you want to avoid and what sort of trouble you are prepared to suffer. Paul advises Timothy to:

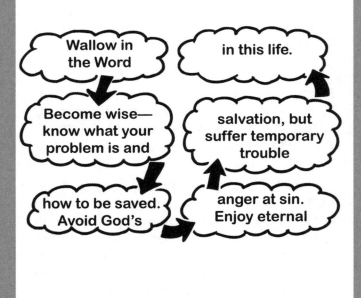

Wallow in the Word

in this life.

Become wise—know what your problem is and

salvation, but suffer temporary trouble

how to be saved. Avoid God's

anger at sin. Enjoy eternal

The alternative is to:

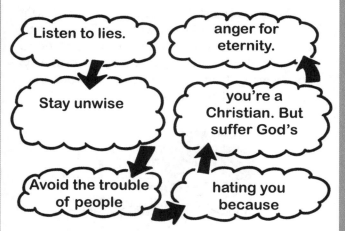

It is in the Bible that we find out who God is, what He thinks of us and that we are in trouble! It is in the Bible that we discover there is a solution. To refresh your memory about the great message of salvation and why we need the Bible to tell us about it—go back to the Safety Notes in chapter 1.

So if the Bible can make me wise for salvation does it follow that if I read it everyday I will be saved? What do you think? No! The answer is No! The Bible can't save you, but it can make you wise for salvation. Imagine you're in a restaurant reading the menu. It won't stop you feeling hungry (in fact it will probably make your mouth water!) but it tells you what is available to sort your hunger out. It makes you wise for ordering and subsequently satisfying your hunger!

Similarly reading a medical book might help you realise what is wrong with you and advise you about what to do, but it won't make you well. It will make you wise for recovery. Even having the right medicine on your shelf won't help until you take it.

As we read God's Word daily we will be inputting wisdom for salvation. We will be keeping the truth uppermost in our minds. Our focus will be shifted back to what our real problem is, what our real need is, *and* what the real answer is.

Are you wise for salvation? It is only God's Word that can help you. Only God can reveal these truths and it is his Word the Bible where we find these written down. Which leads us to our next selling point–they are coming thick and fast now!

SELLING POINT 3

The Bible is God-breathed. Scripture was breathed out by God. It started with God. It isn't that the human authors wrote something off their own back and then God-breathed into what they wrote. In his book on 2nd Timothy John Stott describes it this way: "It originated in God's mind, and was communicated from God's mouth by God's breath or Spirit"[1].

It literally is the Word of God. If we truly accepted that the Bible is God-breathed what sort of position would it have in our daily life? Let's put it another way–think about the time and value you give to the Bible in your day to day life. I'll do it too.

Jo's Notes: Generally daily, but maybe not on a Saturday, quite short, poor concentration, reluctant.

What does that say about the importance I place on the Word breathed out by God? This is God we're talking about. The maker of the universe, the greatest authority, our loving Father, the one with whom we will exist for all eternity or who will judge us for all eternity.

Does the importance you and I give the Bible in our week reflect that we believe it is God-breathed? Does the place you and I

[1] *The Message of 2 Timothy* from the Bible Speaks Today series

give the Bible in our daily lives reflect that we value the Word breathed out by God?

A final thought on this one. Everything we take in to our hearts and minds is breathed out by someone. Think about the things that regularly get your attention. What is it that you would rarely go a day without listening to, reading or watching?

Now ask yourself - who breathes out those 'daily essentials'? Does your life have a bad case of bad breath? Weigh up your inputs – how many come from God, and how many from the world that is opposed to Him? When you look at it this way are you happy with the balance of things?

SELLING POINT 4

The Bible is useful, that is, it is profitable. Now, I'm presuming that most of you reading this aren't great business men and women who spend their days dealing in profit margins and the like. But if we are honest we all like profit.

We all have limited resources–whether that is time, or money or energy. When we commit to something we want to know—is it worth my while? Is the Bible worth my while?

The answer Paul gives is "Yes!" Here is something else that John Stott wrote: "The Bible's divine origin secures and explains its human profit."[2] So what will we get out of it? What sort of profit are we talking about?

PLAY: 2 TIMOTHY 3:16

All Scripture is God-breathed and is useful for teaching, rebuking, correcting and training in righteousness,

Spot four important things that happen when we read the Bible.

We are t_____, c_____,

r_____ and t_____.

Imagine having a makeover. Sorry boys, I'm reading a fashion guru's autobiography at the moment! Your stylist will *teach* you how to think about your wardrobe–you would learn the truth about what suited you, what shape you are, what colours work for you. What to

---

[2] *The Message of 2 Timothy* from the Bible Speaks Today series

accentuate and what to hide. They would *correct* your wrong thinking, reveal the errors in the way you saw yourself and the choices you made. You would be *rebuked* for the terrible things they found in your wardrobe which would be hastily consigned to bin bags or charity shops. Finally, having filled your mind and heart with the right thinking and thrown out all that didn't fit with that, they would *train* you to buy the right clothes and to put together great outfits.

Lots of illustrations would do—we could go back to our healthy eating idea. You are taught the truth about what foods to eat, in what quantities and when. Your wrong thinking about what passes as healthy will be corrected. You will be rebuked for the junk in your fridge and made to chuck it out, then you will be trained to fill them with the right stuff and to get into the best habits.

Naturally our thinking is all wrong. I'm sorry to say it but your brain is not filled with truth. This is how the Bible describes our thinking:

PLAY: READ ROMANS 1:18-23

[18]The wrath of God is being revealed from heaven against all the godlessness and wickedness of people, who suppress the truth by their wickedness, [19]since what may be known about God is plain to them, because God has made it plain to them. [20]For since the creation of the world God's invisible

qualities—His eternal power and divine nature—
have been clearly seen, being understood from
what has been made, so that people are without
excuse.

²¹For although they knew God, they neither
glorified Him as God nor gave thanks to Him, but
their thinking became futile and their foolish hearts
were darkened. ²²Although they claimed to be
wise, they became fools ²³and exchanged the
glory of the immortal God for images made to look
like a mortal human being and birds and animals
and reptiles.

I'm guessing that if you are reading this book
you will have heard some truth in your life, but
it's like our brains are full of leaks, and what
does stay in gets polluted. We need constant
maintenance. As we read the Bible we are
taught truth, our error is corrected, we are
rebuked for the wrong living that comes out
of those errors and trained how to live in line
with the truth. Now that's profit!

Maybe you started reading this book
thinking—why should I? Give me one good
reason why I should read the Bible regularly!
Of course, we might not ever actually say that
to anyone, but we probably think it. Well Paul
gave Timothy some great reasons. Jot down
a couple below.

....

....

Now give me one good reason why you and I shouldn't read the Bible as an immovable part of our daily routines.

Timothy was to go on teaching the truth from God's Word in a climate where that was unpopular, strange and dangerous. The people who heard him faced a choice. You face the same choice today. The choice you and I face when we are battling with whether to spend time reading the Bible each day is will I listen to the truth today or will I listen to myths? To what will I turn my ears? What are my ears itching to hear?

IT'S GOOD TO TALK

How and why should I pray?

THE FINAL Safety Note you signed up to at the start of the book (you did read that bit didn't you?!!) was about prayer. Remember: having a quiet time is not a spectator sport.

But what is prayer? What would you say if someone asked you?

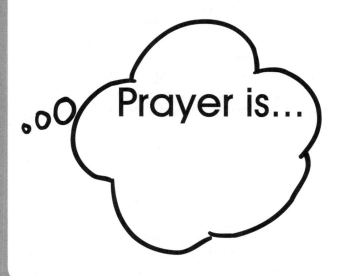

Although prayer is something that most people have tried at least once in their lives it is only God's definition of prayer that matters. After all it is God that we are talking to when we pray. That's what prayer is by the way–talking to, or communicating with God. That is: putting into words either out loud, in our heads, or in writing what we want to say to Him. Not surprised so far? How about this: we can only pray–that is talk to God the Father—because of Jesus and we need to rely totally on Him to help us. Without Jesus prayer is not possible.

So be reassured, prayer is as simple as talking. But don't be fooled by this simplicity.

Stop and think about the physical act of speaking for a moment. While, for most of us, talking is pretty easy; the mechanics and muscles and biology of it all are amazing and complex. Similarly, prayer is simple enough for a toddler to manage, and yet what actually goes on when we pray is profoundly wonderful. The difference is that while we may never really need to know any of the detailed mechanics of speech, it is important to grow more aware of the privilege that is prayer and the price that was paid so we can do it.

Think of someone you can easily talk to—someone you feel comfortable with, someone you can easily get in touch with. Have you thought of someone? Now think of someone who it would be very hard to talk to–both in

terms of not knowing what to say to them and not being able to get in touch with them. Any ideas? Well, I have never tried to get in touch with the Prime Minister or a member of the Royal Family, but if I did pluck up the courage to ring them I don't think they would take my call!

What about talking to God? Is God easy to access and easy to talk to... *or*...scary to talk to and impossible to get in touch with?

Presumably if I were the Prime Minister's child I would find it easy to get in touch with the Prime Minister. So who, if anyone, can dare to utter even a syllable at God's throne? Let's go back to Safety Note Number 1 to help us here.

WHAT IS YOUR STATUS BEFORE GOD?

By nature we are God's enemies. He is perfect, totally without sin and the ruler of the universe. We are sinful rebels. We have no right to talk to Him.

God gave His people a brilliant illustration of this when He gave them instructions to build the temple in the Old Testament. In the temple there was to be a very special area called THE MOST HOLY PLACE. Only the High Priest could go there once a year after some very particular preparations. God set things up this way to teach sinful people that their sin separated them from Him. They couldn't get near. The barrier between the Most Holy Place and the rest of the temple was a massive curtain (and we're not talking about the sort you have in your bedroom—it was 10 centimetres thick and about 20 metres high!) It was as though God put a big *"No Entry"* sign between Him and His people.

But this wasn't the end of the story. God had more to teach His people! At the exact moment Jesus died the curtain tore from top to bottom! The way was open. The *"No Entry"* sign was gone. Jesus' body is like that curtain— it was broken for us to make the way clear for us to be with God. If we believe in the Lord Jesus and accept what He has done for us then we are God's friends. Christians are God's children with every right to run confidently into His throne room day or night.

The writer to the Hebrews wanted his readers to know this. They already knew all about the Old Testament so he uses loads of temple language to explain things. Let's read Hebrews chapter 10:19-23. But first you've got to PAUSE!

ORIENTATION FOR HEBREWS 10:19-22

Hebrews is in the New Testament. Jesus has returned to heaven and His people are learning to live His way while they wait for His return. We don't know who wrote Hebrews, but we do know why. It was written to help people who were in danger of going back to Old Testament rules and regulations and forgetting that salvation comes through God's grace in Jesus. Were they really completely sorted with God because of what Jesus did? The answer Hebrews gives is YES! Did the NO ENTRY sign need to go back up? NO WAY!

PLAY: READ HEBREWS 10:19-22

"Therefore[1], brothers and sisters, since we have confidence to enter the Most Holy Place by the blood of Jesus, by a new and living way opened for us through the curtain, that is His body...let us draw near to God with a sincere heart in full assurance of faith....

---

[1]The writer to the Hebrews has just been talking about the difference that Jesus made.

Wow! So prayer is amazingly simple. It is talking to God. It is also amazingly grace-full. It is an undeserved gift that cost Jesus His life. He opened the way for us to call God Father and talk to Him as His children.

We can start a prayer 'Dear Father God' with confidence because we are coming in Jesus' name–that is as people who love and rely on Jesus.

By the way while we are talking about some of the language of prayer. Ever thought about what Amen means? Find a mirror to check if you're right!

I agree with this prayer.

I accept its truth and consequences.

When it comes to praying, we've only just scratched the surface. There's loads more to learn about prayer. You can read whole books about it—check out the book recommendations in Appendix 1. But our job right now is to think about the role of prayer in our quiet times.

Before we do so, remember–it isn't what we understand about prayer that makes our prayers precious to God. When my babies first started talking I wasn't cross that they didn't do it perfectly. I was excited and pleased that they were communicating with me. Don't worry about getting prayer wrong. We can have complete confidence when we pray to our heavenly Father because of what Jesus has done and because of the help He goes on giving us.

So, this is how I have described a quiet time: It is a specific, planned slot of time in which you can be quiet in order to:

- read a specific passage from the Bible.

- think about it.

- pray about it.

- pray for your day.

- pray for a variety of people and situations.

Prayer needs to come in right at the start as a vital part of your Bible reading.

The Bible is useful for teaching, correcting, rebuking and training, it can make you wise for salvation–but it isn't just an instruction manual or text book that we can take or leave as we like. Reading the Bible is a risky business and it is interactive. Remember how Hebrews 4:12 describes the Bible?

Let's read it and see. But remember— PAUSE!

ORIENTATION

We're back in Hebrews again so refresh your memory using our ORIENTATION! for Hebrews 10 earlier in this chapter. In chapters 3 and 4 the writer to the Hebrews has been urging his readers to learn from what happened to God's people in the Old Testament. As they read God's Word (on this occasion a Psalm) they need to realise it is at work dissecting and revealing their hearts! They can either be saved by it or condemned by what they read.

PLAY: HEBREWS 4:12

"For the word of God is living and active. Sharper than any double-edged sword, it penetrates even to dividing soul and spirit, joints and marrow; it judges the thoughts and attitudes of the heart."

When we read the Word of God, His Spirit[2] speaks to us and we respond. We may not be aware of it–but we do. We never read the Bible neutrally. Our hearts either soften to God's Word or harden to it.

---

[2]The Holy Spirit. The third person of the Trinity: God: Father; Son; and Holy Spirit. For more information see Appendix 2.

- Our basic response is *either* submission
  to God's authority–"Yes Lord, you're in
  charge–I don't understand it all, I need
  to find out more – I didn't get that verse
  at all, but what YOU say goes".

- *Or* rebellion against that authority. "Let's
  see–what do I conclude about all this.
  I don't like that bit, I'm not doing that, I
  won't do anything about this, but this bit
  seems good".

If we are Christians–see Safety Note
Number 1–we have the Holy Spirit in us. It is
the Holy Spirit who helps us respond to the
Spirit-inspired Word of God. We need to pray
for God to work in us as we read His Word.

Have you ever tried to read any of
Shakespeare's plays? Imagine having William
Shakespeare himself sitting next to you as you
read *Hamlet* or *Romeo and Juliet*. We would
be crazy and arrogant not to ask for his help
in understanding it. God is with us as we read
His Word. Ask for His help to discover the heart
of what He is saying.

God is also in us as we read His Word. We
can't hide from Him what we think of what He
says. He knows our response better than we
do. Ask for His help to respond rightly to His
Word in your heart.

Here are the sort of prayers that might be
said as we read the Bible. Think about the role
prayer is playing in this person's Bible reading.

- Before: Thank you for this part of the Bible. Help me to understand it and to know You better as I read it. Please use your Word to make me wise for salvation, to teach me, correct me, rebuke me and train me. In Jesus' name, Amen.

- During: Was that homework meant to be in today–whoops concentrate–Lord please help me to focus on what I'm reading. AND/OR Lord this bit seems totally unfair–help me to understand it and to trust You. Help me to have a chance to ask _____ about it.

- After: This part of the Bible has shown me what You're like: wow.....I praise You... This part of the Bible has shown me what I'm like: ow....I'm sorry.... This part of the Bible is going to change things: now......please help ...

(By the way when you actually pray about a passage of the Bible you have to fill in the blanks here!) So firstly talk to God about His Word, next talk to Him about your day.

While what we pray about from the Bible should be tied to our real lives and will often touch the specifics of our day, a quiet time is also a chance to talk to God more generally about what's going on. The different things on your mind, events, fears, excitements, temptations, worries. What do you think? Would it be easy or strange to pray about the bits and pieces of your life? Here are some reasons why people don't talk to God about the details of their days.

- "God's just not interested in that part of my life!"
- "That's far too small an issue to talk to God about."
- "I've gone so wrong there's no way I can start talking to God about it now."
- "There's no point—God can't do anything about *that*!"
- "That bit has nothing to do with God–it just isn't a 'God thing'!"
- "That's far too embarrassing to pray about!"
- "I know it is wrong, but I've made up my mind. Why bother praying about it?"
- "Talk to God about that? No way! I don't talk to anyone about that."

Underline the ones you might use! Be honest now and jot down any others you can think of. Now look at a couple of Bible passages that will help us chuck out those reasons for good. But first... PAUSE!

ORIENTATION FOR PHILIPPIANS

This is from one of Paul's letters in the New Testament–this time to the church in a place called Philippi. Paul is in prison while he is writing it but that doesn't stop him encouraging and teaching them about their partnership with him in the gospel. This bit comes from near the end of his letter.

PLAY: PHILIPPIANS 4:6

"Do not be anxious about anything, but in everything, by prayer and petition, with thanksgiving, present your requests to God."

Next stop Colossians. But PAUSE!

ORIENTATION FOR COLOSSIANS

Colossians is another of Paul's letters, this time to the Christians in a place called Colossae.

PLAY: COLOSSIANS 3:17

"And whatever you do, whether in word or deed, do it all in the name of the Lord Jesus, giving thanks to God the Father through Him."

PLAY: HEBREWS CHAPTER 10:19-22

"Therefore, brothers, since we have confidence to enter the Most Holy Place by the blood of Jesus, by a new and living way opened for us through the curtain, that is His body............let us draw near to God with a sincere heart in full assurance of faith....

If you are a Christian you are to live every second of your day as a Christian, to show how great God is, *and* there isn't one part of your life that you can't talk to Him about: no matter how small and insignificant; private or embarrassing; no matter how sinful and terrible. All of it matters to God and the way is always open. So does God agree with your worries, excuses and refusals on page 85? Of course not! So go on—open the bin and

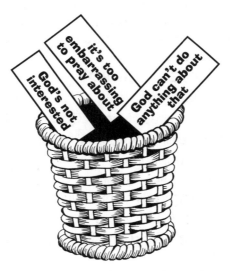

chuck them in! Are you encouraged to talk through your day with God? What truths from God's Word have helped?

The third and final role I want to mention about praying in our quiet times is praying for a variety of people and situations.

The day ahead of you or what you have just read in the Bible may bring to mind certain people and situations. Great! Get talking to God about it. But it is also important to be proactive about it. Without a bit of planning some people or events may never get prayed for! A quiet time gives us a slot of time in which to pray in an organised way. Who or what do you want to talk to God about regularly? In case you've gone blank here's a list of some of the people/things that other Christians have on their list of prayer points. This is to give you a flavour—it is not a list you have to use from beginning to end!

- YOUR LOCAL CHURCH

  The leaders

  Faithful preaching of God's Word

  Particular events coming up

  Your youth group

  Missionaries, or other Christian groups supported by your church

- THE WORLD

  Christians and Christian ministry around the world

  Places of particular suffering

- PEOPLE

  Your family

  Christian friends

  Friends who are not Christians

  People you know in difficulty

- YOUR SCHOOL/WORKPLACE

People you find difficult

Opportunities for the good news about Jesus to be shared

So, are you interested in a daily habit of prayer? Well make a start!

- Step 1: pray around and through your Bible reading.

- Step 2: talk to God about your day.

- Step 3: plan to pray regularly for certain people and situations.

We're not finished with prayer—look out for some practical pointers in chapter 8 and think with me about God's priorities for our prayers in the next chapter. But for now an important reminder: while it is good and right to mature in our prayer lives; our toddler like utterances are just as beautiful to God as our best informed and most planned prayers.

LORD, TEACH US TO PRAY

God's priorities for our prayers

HAVE YOU started to get an idea of what prayer is and how amazing it is that prayer is even possible? Have you had a few ideas about what and who to pray about? Great! Then you should be asking a very obvious question: "What do I actually say?"

Of course with situations well known to you what to pray for will often seem pretty obvious. With some of your friends and family it may be possible to simply ask them how you can pray for them. For prayer topics further afield you may be able to get hold of a book, website or prayer letter which lists items for prayer. But no matter how much information we have we mustn't ignore this vital question: "What is on God's heart for these people and situations?"

Imagine it's Monday morning. You prayed for God's help and then read Psalm 1. After you might pray something along the lines of:

- Wow: Dear Father God, You give Your people Your wonderful law and You watch over their ways.

- Ow: I'm sorry that I so often listen to what sinners have to say and ignore your Word. Like the other day when........ Please forgive me because Jesus died for me.

- Now: Thank You that I've made time today to read the Bible and pray – help me to do this again tomorrow. Help me to turn to your Word more regularly. In Jesus' name, Amen.

You move from praying specifically about Psalm 1 to talking to God about the specifics of your day. This is what comes to mind:

1. Help! I have Mr _____ first lesson this morning. He picks on me.

2. We're doing such and such in science and I'm working with so and so. At least that lesson won't be so painful.

3. Mum picks me up on a Monday–I love not having to walk home.

4. I wonder if I'll manage to tell people anything about youth group when they ask me how my weekend was?

How does God want you to talk to Him about all that?

Finally, let's imagine that, as well as praying about your Bible reading and your day, you have decided to pray for one other person each week day. On a Monday (in our completely made up scenario) you pray for your friend _____. You're not sure if he/she is a Christian but they have been coming along to your church with you most weeks. You're aware that they are very quiet about it at school though and tend to go along with the crowd. If you asked God to teach you to pray for this friend what would He say?

The disciples (Jesus' followers) asked Jesus to teach them to pray—this is what He said... but remember—PAUSE!

ORIENTATION FOR MATTHEW

The Lord's prayer (as we often call it now) was recorded by Matthew in his book about Jesus. Matthew gives us a number of chunks of teaching from Jesus and here in chapter 6 we are in the middle of the first one. This chunk is known as the Sermon on the Mount and it comes just after Matthew has told us about Jesus' birth and how He started His earthly ministry.

PLAY: MATTHEW 6:9-13

⁹"This, then, is how you should pray:

'Our Father in heaven,

hallowed be your name,

¹⁰your kingdom come,

your will be done,

on earth as it is in heaven.

¹¹Give us today our daily bread.

¹²And forgive us our debts,

as we also have forgiven our debtors.

¹³And lead us not into temptation,

but deliver us from the evil one.'"

Now you may be wondering how helpful Jesus' answer is. What has all that got to do with our imaginary Monday morning prayer session? After all–it's more of a formal prayer we say all together in church—isn't it?

No! This prayer shows us what's on God's heart for us and for the world we live in. This prayer shows us what God is longing to hear from His people.

LESSON 1

Our Father in heaven

When a Christian prays he or she can call God Father. Father sounds formal and distant to us – but the disciples would have been amazed at the intimacy. The disciples were Jews and would have been very aware that God was perfect and separate from sinful humanity. They wouldn't even utter His name. But now because they are following Jesus they can talk directly to Him as their Dad, their Father.

LESSON 2

Hallowed be your name, your kingdom come, your will be done on earth as it is in heaven.

What do you tend to put at the top of your list when you talk to your Father God? What should we put there? In fact what should be top of our list all the time?

The Lord's prayer teaches us that it is our Father's REPUTATION (what people think of Him and how they speak of Him) and His RULE (people's obedience to Him) that should be our top priority at all times.

LESSON 3

Give us today our daily bread.

Next we are taught to RELY on our Father. As we pray we can be sure that He will give us everything we need today.

LESSON 4

Forgive us our debts, as we also have forgiven our debtors. And lead us not into temptation but deliver us from the evil one.

'Our Father' isn't just a way to start a prayer–Christians are in a *relationship* with God. Here we are taught to pray about this relationship, to ask for forgiveness of our debts (or sins). These sins spoil our relationship with God, but in Jesus they can be completely cleared away. We should be daily asking God to keep us from walking into temptation – situations where sin is likely to call to us even more loudly than usual. We need God's help to avoid and resist the temptations that come our way. The devil wants to break our relationship with God, but God is more powerful. All we need to do is admit the reality of evil and ask for our Father to keep us safe.

LESSON 5

For yours is the kingdom, the power and the glory for ever and ever, Amen.

You won't see this bit in the passage above because it does not appear in the original texts that we have of Jesus' teaching. It is, however, a great pattern to follow in our prayers: Rejoicing in; Remembering; Recognising;and Resting in our Fathers' splendour.

Over to you:

1. Who would you say is the star of this prayer? Who is it about?

2. When our lives get prayed about in this prayer, what is the key issue that Jesus teaches us to pray about?

Let's get back to our imaginary Monday morning. Remember: if you are a follower of Jesus you are bringing your Bible reading, your day and your friend to your Father God in prayer. He is longing to listen and powerful to act. God hears you because you are His child (not because of how you've been behaving lately.) All this is only possible because of Jesus.

If you look back to chapter 5 at the sample prayers from Psalm 1 you'll see that the prayers we prayed were clearly centred on God, our relationship with Him and His rule in our lives. We asked forgiveness for our sin and asked for God's help to live His way.

How can we keep that focus when we come to pray about that history lesson first thing? Well, a Christian's main desire in this situation should be that God would be shown to be wonderful and that God's ways would be followed.

Remember it's God's reputation and rule and our relationship with Him that are most important. So with this in mind which of the following things would be good to ask God for?

Dear Father God please,

1. Make my teacher ill today.
2. Help me to be patient when things are unfair.
3. May my teacher act fairly.
4. Help me not to speak unkindly of the teacher to my friends.
5. Stop me thinking nasty thoughts.
6. Help my teacher to find out about Jesus, to see something different about my reactions because I am a Christian.
7. Please make my teacher pick on someone else.
8. Help me forgive my teacher.
9. Help me to trust You when it is hard.
10. Give me someone trustworthy to talk and pray about it with.

Cross out the two that go against the lessons that we learnt in the Lord's prayer.

What about when someone asks you about your weekend? How could your prayers keep the focus on God here?

Why not ask God for courage, the right words to say so that God's greatness and His right to rule would be spoken of. Ask for protection from the desire to lie about what you have done. And don't forget the more positive parts of the day! Thank your Father in heaven who gives you everything you need and often so much more.

Excellent. We've prayed about our Bible reading, we've talked to God about our day. Now what about praying for our friend. What does the Lord's prayer show us to be God's main focus for our prayers here?

Here are some ideas I have come up with for the imaginary friend we mentioned earlier.

- Thank God that they have been coming to youth group.
- Ask God that they would know God as their Father and that they would want other people to know how great God is.
- Ask God to help you to be a good friend to them and an example. Ask God to show your friend that what you learn on Sunday makes a difference to life on Monday.

These are just examples of course – but can you see that although the prayer that Jesus taught His friends didn't mention Psalm 1, your teacher or your friend, it does teach you what should be top of your list when praying for these sorts of things?

Did you know that there are lots of prayers already written for us in the Bible that can help us to remember what's really important? PAUSE! We need some... ORIENTATION.

ORIENTATION: PAUL'S LETTERS

These verses all come from letters that Paul wrote either to an individual or to a church in a particular place. We are not in identical situations but as Christians living in the world after Jesus' ascension to heaven and before His return we are basically serving God in a pretty similar context. The job of the people that Paul wrote to was to faithfully live God's way and to share the good news about Jesus. We are to do the same. Our prayers for those who love Jesus, for our churches, for missionaries telling people about Jesus, for Christians going through a hard time... can be taken straight from these prayers that Paul prayed many, many years ago.

Here are some prayers for people as they share the good news about Jesus.

PLAY: EPHESIANS 6:19-20

[19]Pray also for me, that whenever I speak, words may be given me so that I will fearlessly make known the mystery of the gospel, [20]for which I am an ambassador in chains. Pray that I may declare it fearlessly, as I should.

PLAY: COLOSSIANS 4:2-4

²Devote yourselves to prayer, being watchful and thankful. ³And pray for us, too, that God may open a door for our message, so that we may proclaim the mystery of Christ, for which I am in chains. ⁴Pray that I may proclaim it clearly, as I should.

Here is a prayer for world leaders/ situations and for non-Christians.

PLAY: 1 TIMOTHY 2:1-4

²I urge, then, first of all, that petitions, prayers, intercession and thanksgiving be made for all people—for kings and all those in authority, that we may live peaceful and quiet lives in all godliness and holiness. ³This is good, and pleases God our Saviour, ⁴who wants all people to be saved and to come to a knowledge of the truth.

Here is a great prayer for unity in a church.

PLAY: ROMANS 15:5-6

⁵May the God who gives endurance and encouragement give you the same attitude of mind toward each other that Christ Jesus had, ⁶so that with one mind and one voice you may glorify the God and Father of our Lord Jesus Christ.

Here we have some more general prayers for Christians in all sorts of situations.

PLAY: ROMANS 15:13

¹³May the God of hope fill you with all joy and peace as you trust in Him, so that you may overflow with hope by the power of the Holy Spirit.

PLAY: 1 CORINTHIANS 16:23

[23]The grace of the Lord Jesus be with you.

PLAY: EPHESIANS 1:15-19

[15]For this reason, ever since I heard about your faith in the Lord Jesus and your love for all God's people, [16]I have not stopped giving thanks for you, remembering you in my prayers. [17]I keep asking that the God of our Lord Jesus Christ, the glorious Father, may give you the Spirit of wisdom and revelation, so that you may know Him better. [18]I pray that the eyes of your heart may be enlightened in order that you may know the hope to which He has called you, the riches of His glorious inheritance in His holy people, [19]and His incomparably great power for us who believe.

PLAY: EPHESIANS 3:14-19

[14]For this reason I kneel before the Father, [15]from whom every family in heaven and on earth derives its name. [16]I pray that out of His glorious riches He may strengthen you with power through his Spirit in your inner being, [17]so that Christ may dwell in your hearts through faith. And I pray that you, being rooted and established in love, [18]may have power, together with all the Lord's holy people, to grasp how wide and long and high and deep is the love of Christ, [19]and to know this love that surpasses knowledge—that you may be filled to the measure of all the fullness of God.

PLAY: PHILIPPIANS 1:9-11

[9]And this is my prayer: that your love may abound more and more in knowledge and depth of insight, [10]so that you may be able to discern what

is best and may be pure and blameless for the day of Christ, ¹¹filled with the fruit of righteousness that comes through Jesus Christ—to the glory and praise of God.

PLAY: 1 THESSALONIANS 5:23-24

²³May God Himself, the God of peace, sanctify you through and through. May your whole spirit, soul and body be kept blameless at the coming of our Lord Jesus Christ. ²⁴The one who calls you is faithful, and He will do it.

PLAY: 2 THESSALONIANS 2:16-17

¹⁶May our Lord Jesus Christ Himself and God our Father, who loved us and by His grace gave us eternal encouragement and good hope, ¹⁷encourage your hearts and strengthen you in every good deed and word.

These verses should remind us of the same lessons that we were taught by the Lord's prayer. Paul's concern as he prays is for God's rule and reputation, for his readers to rely on God, and for their relationship with God.

So am I saying that you can ignore the exam your friend is terrified about, the flu they are suffering from or the fact that they are being bullied? No! God doesn't want us to ignore the lives being lived and the world they are being lived in. No—pray for people specifically and in the context of their everyday lives. The prayers from the Bible we have been reading don't push out the detail–they tell us what to pray for in the detail.

It's the same as you pray about your life. If you are God's child your heart is one of God's priorities. Your heart is on His heart. What takes up your heart space? Think of what excites you, what worries you, what you are obsessed with, what you keep secret....

How many of these things do you pray about? While our prayers need to reflect God's heart, they also need to reflect our hearts. If they don't we are not relating to God in our prayers. As we grow more like Jesus, our hearts will increasingly have God as the star–and that will be reflected in prayers full of God's priorities. The only place to start of course is to get talking to God about the things that you have on your heart now.

When we do bring the longings or fears of our hearts to God we can sometimes regret that God is not a genie and our prayers like Aladdin's wishes. But if we think about it–we should be very glad that this isn't the case. When we pray God always listens, but He always stays in charge. We are not the master commanding, but the child asking. Quite regularly we are foolish children asking a wise Father for harmful or wrongly timed gifts. I can think of many prayers that I prayed for with all my heart that–looking back—I am very glad God didn't answer as I wanted. For example

I prayed and prayed that I would marry a particular man. I tagged on the end—if it is Your will God, but I knew what I wanted and what I thought God's will should be! But it wasn't God's will. With time, the help of wise friends and the way the situation developed my prayers changed to be more centred on what God wanted. I asked for God to do what was best for me in my relationship with God and to give me a willingness to see and accept that. And I thank Him (and I presume the man I DID marry does too!) that He answered that prayer.

In your prayers make God and His kingdom the star. Plan well so that you pray wisely for His work in this world—but don't neglect your heart or your life. As well as planning to pray, just pray a lot. As we read in the last chapter, Paul urges us:

"Do not be anxious about anything, but in everything, by prayer and petition, with thanksgiving, present your requests to God. And the peace of God, which surpasses all understanding, will guard your hearts and your minds in Christ Jesus." Philippians 4:6-7

When it comes to eating we are encouraged to eat planned meals and not snack between them. Prayer is NOT like that. You can feast on a full English breakfast prayer slot first thing and then snack on quick 'Thank You!' or 'Help' or 'Sorry' prayers as much as you like!

This brings me to my final point. Make sure you have a good balanced diet in your prayers.

What different types of prayers can you think of that you should include? Have you heard of teaspoon prayers? When a recipe wants you to use a teaspoon of something it abbreviates it to tsp. In prayer we can use this to remind us to say thank you, sorry and please.

If that is a bit simple for you—try this. The language isn't easy, but it is rich. RC Sproul writes: "Charles Hodge declared that 'prayer is the converse of the soul with God. In and through prayer we express our reverence and adoration for God; we bare our souls in contrite confession before Him; we pour out the thanksgiving of grateful hearts; and we offer our petitions and supplications to Him.'[1]

We can summarise this with the letters: ACTS.

- Adoration
- Confession
- Thanksgiving
- Supplication

ADORATION

As Jesus taught us in the Lord's prayer–we start with God and how wonderful He is. Our main purpose is to 'glorify God and enjoy Him forever'. Declare in your prayers how amazing God is. Praise Him. This is the purpose of the WOW prayer from our Bible reading. We can plan to adore God in our daily prayers by having a different attribute or characteristic of God for each day of the week.

For example: God's *Might* or *Mercy* on a Monday, His *Trustworthiness* on a Tuesday,

---

[1] RC Sproul in *Essential Truths of the Christian Faith* (page 261) Published by Tyndale Copyright 1992.

His *Wisdom* or *Worth* on a Wednesday, His *Threefold Nature* on a Thursday, His *Fatherliness* on a Friday, His *Saving Nature* on a Saturday and a Sunday.

As you praise God try to stay focussed on what He is like rather than on how that affects us. (This is what makes *Praise* prayers different from *Thank You* prayers.)

CONFESSION

This is another way of reminding us that we need to say sorry to God. It will often be prompted by what we have read in the Bible. We can also ask the Holy Spirit to show us from our lives what we need to say sorry for. There will be things missing from our lives as well as things that are there but shouldn't be.

THANKSGIVING

This one is easy to understand but do we actually do it? I can be slow to thank God for all the prayers He answers. I forget to thank Him for all the blessings He gives me. We all need to be more thankful to our wonderful Heavenly Father. And finally...

SUPPLICATION

You might not use this word much but as far as prayer is concerned it's probably the type of prayer we're most familiar with... asking God for things. Think shopping list if the word supplication is too complicated. But remember that the things that are on God's shopping list are the best things to ask Him for.

So make sure your praying praises and thanks God, says sorry to Him and calls out to Him for things.

Did you start this chapter asking: "What do I actually say to God?"

Well, I hope you now have:

- a taste for what God wants you to pray about

- a hunger to pray for everything from the daily bits and pieces of life to your heart's desires and fears and

- a menu plan for a balanced diet of prayer.

We're off now to tackle some excuses!

P.S. Don't forget to check out the ideas for further reading about prayer in Appendix 1.

AND finally....just before we move on please try out my tricky questions

1.   I can pray confidently because.....

b.   my parents are Christians

c.   I don't swear

d.   Jesus made it possible

2.   To get into heaven I need to pray for....

a.   5 minutes a day

b.   10 minutes twice a day

c.   other people and not just myself

3.   I can only pray if...

a.   I have brushed my teeth

b.   I understand everything about prayer

c.   I am God's child because of Jesus

Answers:

1.   c

2.   none of them, they are all rubbish

3.   c

Basically – remember Safety Note Number 1. Get grace and don't forget it.

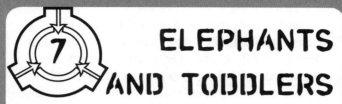

ELEPHANTS AND TODDLERS

Tackling a few excuses

SO HERE are some excuses people give for not having a quiet time:

- I'm too busy, I'm too tired, it's too hard, I've read it all before...

Wait a minute. *Stop!* Why am I giving you ideas? I'm trying to get you to tackle your excuses not put new ones into your head. You tell me. What are the excuses you can come up with for not having a quiet time?

Now think back to what you have read from God's Word and about God's Word. Remember what prayer is and why it is so important. Go on–tackle those excuses to the ground. If you need help chat about it with a wise friend, leader or parent. Believe me– they will have had to tackle some of the same excuses themselves. In fact if they have had a quiet time this morning they will have had to knock one or two over today!

So where do the elephants and toddlers come in?

Well....imagine a pool of water. Next to it are standing an elephant and a toddler. Despite both being dirty, smelly and hot—neither fancy taking the plunge. The elephant comes up with this excuse. "I couldn't possibly go in there–I am so large–it is probably far too shallow for me." The toddler's excuse is quite different. "Well I can't go in–it may go right over my head I am so small."

When you consider setting out on your own reading the Bible and praying which do you feel like—the elephant or the toddler? Is your worry that a quiet time would be far too shallow? Perhaps you have been going to Sunday school or youth club and having family times praying and reading the Bible all of your life. Do you feel familiar with most of the 'main' stories in the Bible? Perhaps you know the answers to the questions before you even

look up the passage. Is it possible to simply grow out of reading the Bible and praying?

Well I'm sure you know what I'm going to say. Just in case you're wondering I'll give you a clue: it starts with an N and it ends in a big fat O. So how can we tackle the following excuses?

- It's childish, it's just too easy, I've done it all before, I know all the answers already, I've grown out of it...

Remember Timothy?

ORIENTATION FOR TIMOTHY

Paul wrote to Timothy about sticking to the truth. He told him how hard it is and how valuable. Although Timothy was a young man, he was leading churches and entrusted with passing on accurate teaching. He also trained believers to teach others. He had been reading the Scriptures from infancy with his mother and grandmother (2 Timothy 1:5 and 3:14). So does Paul say to Timothy: "OK, you've got enough out of scripture now. Start using your time for something different." Well, go on—grab a Bible, check in the contents where 2 Timothy is and use the chapter and verse numbers to find 2 Timothy 3:12-4:5[1].

---

[1] If this is just not possible right now look back at pages 63-65 in chapter 4.

These are the things that jump out at me:

- 3:14 *"Continue"*.
- 3:15 which *"are able"* (not were once able)
- 3:16, 17 almost every word in these verses!
- In chapter 4 Paul charges Timothy to *"keep"* preaching the Word and to *"be ready"* in season and out of season.

Now look up Hebrews 4:12. It should be familiar!

The Bible is not a read once and put it on the shelf sort of book. The Bible is living and active. It is described as a sword used by God to pierce us each time we read it. You know when you read the Bible and God points out something that needs changed in your life. That's the sword of God's Word piercing you.

It is also a sword which we need to wield skilfully. It is part of our Christian armour. Have you heard of the armour of God? Paul describes it at the end of his letter to some Christians in a place called Ephesus.

ORIENTATION FOR EPHESUS

Paul started his letter by reminding them of the good news about Jesus. He's told them what their new lives should look like now they are Christians. Then he warns them that they are in a battle. Not a physical one, but a spiritual one. God's enemy, the Devil, does not want us following, trusting in and being rescued by Jesus. So he attacks us. The good news Paul gives his readers is that a Christian has everything necessary to keep them safe. We have the armour of God because of what Jesus has done. Let's find out more...

PLAY: EPHESIANS 6:10-13 AND 17.

[10]Finally, be strong in the Lord and in His mighty power. [11]Put on the full armour of God, so that you can take your stand against the devil's schemes. [12]For our struggle is not against flesh and blood, but against the rulers, against the authorities, against the powers of this dark world and against the spiritual forces of evil in the heavenly realms. [13]Therefore put on the full armour of God, so that when the day of evil comes, you may be able to stand your ground, and after you have done everything, to stand.

Paul goes on to list the full armour of God, but we're going to skip to the only weapon he mentions.

[17] and the sword of the Spirit, which is the Word of God.

What is our only weapon in this battle? Paul calls it the sword of the Spirit – but what is that? It's the Word of God or the Bible. So can we start to leave it behind as we grow up? No way! Surely the more experienced a soldier is the less likely they are to leave their weapon behind when they go into battle! Similarly the longer you're a Christian the more you will realise how much you need the input of God's Word.

There are lots of other passages we could look at to persuade us that Bible reading is not just for babies. Remember the Psalms we read in chapter 2 and their strong flavour of life long meditation on God's Word?

In fact if you still feel like that elephant– the best thing to do is to take the plunge into the Bible and find out how deep it is. You may re-explore a passage you have 'swum' around before. Push yourself to read it more thoroughly, to find out more about the context of the verses, to do something about what you have read and pass it on to someone else. You may swim into completely unknown waters. You may find a chunk of the Bible that is either completely new or that you have never understood.

Either way the Bible is deep enough for any elephant to plunge into. Do you know any people who have been Christians for a lot longer than you? Do they still read the Bible and pray regularly? Without actually calling them elephants ask them why they still bother and when they imagine they will have finished.

I got in touch with some people who not only have been Christians longer than I have, but who are what we might call the experts. One is a Bishop in the Church of England, one is the leader of two churches, both have written and spoken about Christianity in all sorts of situations—often to other preachers and leaders. This is what they said when I asked them about Bible reading:

"Over the years (and I've been a Christian for over 45 of them!) I have never found it easy to make time for prayer and Bible study. But by God's grace I have persevered – and now know that these two things are not 'luxuries'; they are essentials, and I simply can't manage without them. The more I study the Bible, the more I discover about God and about life; and the more I pray, the more I learn to rely on God. So my message would be: However hard you find it – never give up!"

"The more I go on in the Christian life, the more I see the importance of having a daily time of prayer and Bible study. God reminds us in His Word that his desire for us is to become more like Jesus. As we read the Bible we are taught, corrected, encouraged and rebuked. I constantly find that I need to be corrected by the Word or that I have simply missed a great truth which is sitting there in front of me. It takes humility and courage to place ourselves under God's Word, but it is a constant source of joy and delight. And because it is God's Word I know that I need God's help, not only to understand it correctly, but also to obey it. I once read that 'in His Word God discloses his truth and by prayer he asks us to do it.' So prayer is the other key ingredient to that daily time with God. I need to ask for his help, thank Him for His goodness and bring the needs of the world, the church I serve and my family before Him each day.

"I can't say that it is always easy. Sometimes it is the last thing I want to do, but it is always the first thing I need to do. The fact that it can be such a struggle is testimony that it lies at the heart of the spiritual battle in which we are all engaged – to be God's people and to make God known in the world."

So tackle the poor excuse that you've done it all before. Knock it to the ground! Think about whether you need to stretch yourself a bit more. Which books of the Bible haven't you looked at before? Are you using Bible reading notes that are too young for you or just too familiar? How could you develop your prayer diary to incorporate some of the ideas we looked at in chapters five and six? Read the practical hints and tips in the next chapter and use them to go deeper. *But* at the end of the day if we are finding prayer and Bible study too easy then the problem is with us and not with the Bible or the God we pray to.

- "Hold on! That's not my problem at all. My problem is that I'm not an expert. I'm nowhere near being an expert. I haven't got a clue, it's all far too hard. What if I get it wrong?"

Remember that toddler standing next to the elephant? His worry is that the water will go way over his head. If a quiet time is deep enough for an elephant to dive into can it be shallow enough for a toddler to paddle in?

The wonderful answer to that question is *Yes!* Which means that "It's too hard" is not a good excuse either.

When we learnt about prayer we found out that we can call God–*Dad*–and why?–because of Jesus. A quiet time is not an exam or a piece of coursework. It is time with our heavenly Dad. He loves and accepts us as we are and He will help us to develop.

He will help us by His Spirit[1]. The Holy Spirit is the helper of all Christians–God living in us and with us. Reassuringly the help He gives us is not dependent on our understanding of Him. Rather we simply need to understand and accept that *we* are dependent on *Him*. We can ask God for His help and He will give it.

He will also help us by His people. Which of God's people can help you? Start off by

There is more information about the Holy Spirit in Appendix 2 and further reading ideas in Appendix 1.

thinking locally–who in your family, or your church family can help you? Can they recommend notes you can get to guide you through your Bible reading? Can they answer the questions you have? Can they help you get into a good routine with your prayers? Can they text or call you to remind you to have a quiet time? Do you have Christian friends further afield who can play a similar role? God has not left you alone in this. Christians all around the world and throughout history are working (or have worked) to understand the Bible better and to communicate it to others. When we read a good Christian book or use notes that someone has put together – God is using His people to help you.

Can you remember learning to swim? Were you the super cautious type who took three weeks of lessons to get your feet wet? Or were you more like my youngest son who would quite happily jump into the deep end with nothing to keep him afloat, relying totally on a parent to scoop him up from the depths?

However you go about it there is one basic requirement to learning to swim. You have to get wet. People may be there to paddle with you at the edge, to blow up your water wings, to fish you out, to catch you when you jump/ fall in–but unless the toddler at the edge of the pool gets wet they aren't going to learn to swim.

If you feel like that toddler at the edge of the water let me assure you that you are safe to paddle, to make a start.

So are you an elephant or a toddler? Or does it depend what day it is? Well whatever excuse you're using at the moment keep it flattened. Look back at what we have already covered in this book and read on for some practical hints and tips, but above all remember this: Your main help in all this is the Lord. It is by His strength that we will start and continue a habit of quiet times. It is by His grace that we can come back to it after failing again and again. It is His hand that helps us up off the ground when the excuses have tackled us!

Stop and pray now for His help. Use this prayer that the writer to the Hebrews prays for his readers as he finishes his letter to them.

PLAY: HEBREWS 13:20-21 [1]

[20]Now may the God of peace, who through the blood of the eternal covenant brought back from the dead our Lord Jesus, that great Shepherd of the sheep, [21]equip you with everything good for doing His will, and may He work in us what is pleasing to Him, through Jesus Christ, to whom be glory for ever and ever. Amen.

---

[1] Go back to chapter 5 for your Hebrews ORIENTATION.

Before we move on—one final warning about excuses and an advert for chapter 9.

WARNING!

Don't let your choices masquerade (that's disguise themselves) as excuses.

For example we say "I'm too busy"—which is an excuse. But if we unwrap the excuse we'll find a bunch of choices inside. Like a pass the parcel. What our hearts and minds are really saying is "I don't want to. This is less important than... or I would rather....." When an excuse pops up–unmask it and reveal the choice hiding below. In chapter 9 we'll consider some of those choices we face and perhaps are making without realising it, but for now let's get really practical.

TILTING THE GLASS

Some practical pointers to

get you started and to keep you going

HAVE YOU ever had difficulty filling up a glass with a fizzy drink? You know—there's a line of people behind you waiting to get some too—you hastily pour yourself a glass—but it's all foam. By the time you get back to your seat the foam has bubbled away and you've only got two mouthfuls left.

Hot Tip: Tilt the glass as you pour and you'll get more pop and less foam.

A lot of things in life go more smoothly if we just get the right hints and tips. For example–a quiet time. Have you got your head round the idea of a quiet time yet? Here's how we've been describing it. It's a specific, planned slot of time in which you can be quiet in order to:

- read a specific passage from the Bible.
- think about it.
- pray about it.
- pray for your day.
- pray for various people and situations.

So what's likely to be tricky about this? What is going to get in the way and make it harder? What is the foam that is going to leave no room for the drink and how do we tilt the glass?

Here is some of the froth and foam that have filled my quiet time glass in the past. Is it only me–or do any sound familiar?

- You come to have a quiet time, but your mind goes blank. You ask yourself "What am I meant to be doing again?"
- You get distracted by things going on around you or by all the things whirring round in your head.
- You come across something you don't understand and you don't know how to move on.

- You never know which bit of the Bible to read–you've tried starting at the beginning and reading it all through–but you just end up reading the first half of Genesis again and again.
- You can't remember where you got to last time you read the Bible or what you prayed for last time you prayed.
- Something else always crops up just as you are about to start.
- You can't concentrate.
- It takes you all the time you have put aside to find your Bible and prayer diary.
- You can't think who or what to pray for.
- You can't remember God's priorities for your prayers and you don't want to get it wrong.
- You just fall asleep.

OK, so that's a lot of froth. The good news is we're not starting from scratch. Remember the practical steps we considered in chapter 3? Let's recap.

- Step 1: Ask God to help you: now as you make plans; each time you start a quiet time; and each time you realise you have missed a quiet time... and ...
- Step 2: Plan well. When will you do it? Where will you do it? How long can you realistically plan to spend on it? Make sure you have thought about any factors that will vary through the week.

I think it would be really great if you could write down your plans now. Pray for God's help and then fill in the plan below—or use a separate piece of paper if you prefer

GENERAL QT PLAN

Starting at _____

Need to finish by _____

Best place:

Things that I need to do to make this happen:

Likely problems/distractions and ways around them:

Days when this won't work and alternative plan:

Have you written something down? Don't worry I'm not going to mark it! In fact there isn't really a right or wrong set of answers. The Bible doesn't tell us how long, what time or where. To make a plan isn't to set up the only way you'll ever do a quiet time. Getting the 'right' plan won't give you a place in heaven (think grace!) Having a longer quiet time doesn't earn you more points. At the same time though your plan should reflect the place you want your relationship with God to have in your life.

Most of us don't have an unlimited supply of money. So we budget–we look at what we have, we list the things we would like to use it for and how much they cost and we make choices. Getting one thing means not getting something else. Time is just the same. Make your choices, make a plan.

So what do you need to do to make this happen? Are there people who can help you? Maybe someone who can text you to remind you, or ask you once a week or month how things are going? Do you need to chat to any family members who could help practically by giving you some space for a few minutes, have custody of distracting items such as mobile phones, wake you up earlier or change when breakfast is or the running order of the morning/after school time....

What practical things do you need to sort out? Do you need a Bible? Where is the best place to keep your Bible? (This might seem a bit ridiculous–but remember that we are worms wriggling on a hook and not deep sea divers. Our natural tendency is to not have a quiet time and we need all the help we can get.) What else do you need to have at hand? If you choose to use Bible reading notes (we will talk about those in a minute) you will need them accessible as well as whatever system you choose for prayer (again coming soon in a chapter 8 near you...). Make sure any notebooks or prayer lists/cards and a pencil/pen are within easy reach.

Is there anything that should not be within easy reach? You may need to turn things off or leave them elsewhere. You know the things that distract you—just get rid of them!

Now, remember this list from chapter 3? We got rid of points 2-5 and 9 which left us with:

- Get on with it and make a start.
- ~~Put it off until after exams or holidays or whatever.~~
- ~~Wait until you know a bit more about it.~~
- ~~Tell no one so no one will know if you're struggling.~~
- ~~Tell everyone so they will know how brilliant you are.~~
- Encourage a friend to make a start with you so you can help each other.
- Tell an older Christian and give them permission to check up on you.
- Keep reading this book to find out more about it (You're nearly there with this one!).
- ~~Be pleased that finally you can be sure that you will go to heaven now you are having a quiet time.~~

- Get grace, keep it in mind and don't forget it. Remember Safety Note Number 1—go on read it again!

So what are you waiting for? The next step is really just to take the first step. Well almost. I did promise to give you some pointers on Bible reading notes and prayer lists first—so here they are—but they come with a warning.

WARNING: Don't wait until you have the perfect system in place. Make a start and then go from there.

So you've made a plan and stuck to it. You've dealt with the people and the practicalities, you've prayed for God's help and you are ready to open up that Bible that was waiting for you in just the right place. NOW WHAT?!

QUESTIONS YOU MAY HAVE

- How do I choose which bit to read each day?

- Once I have read something what do I do next?

- How do I know I have understood it properly?

- How do I make sure I remember it and it makes a difference in my life?

One answer (though not the only answer) is *Bible Reading Notes*. In Appendix 1 there are some recommendations for you and information on how to order them.

Good Bible reading notes will give you a bit of the Bible to read each day. They will ask you some questions to help you think about what you have just read. They will explain how God's Word can make a difference to your life and how to pray about it.

I really recommend using Bible reading notes. But don't let them do all the work. Good Bible reading notes will give you more confidence in reading the Bible well–they shouldn't make you feel less able to handle God's Word by yourself. They won't just tell you what they think–they will get you to think about what you are reading. Always remember it is the Bible that is perfect and God-breathed–not the Bible reading notes. Let's re-cap a few of the skills we have gained already then you can use those to make sure your notes are doing a good job or even have a go without notes occasionally.

Firstly–get orientated. Because of the way the Bible has been put together it is generally best to focus on reading one book at a time, rather than jumping in and out of several books. This way you can do your ORIENTATION as you start and follow the flow of the book as you read through it. However, sometimes it is good to focus on what the Bible has to say about a particular topic. This tends to involve looking at a different part of the Bible each time. When you're doing this kind of Bible study please be particularly careful to do your ORIENTATION each time you dive into a different part of the Bible or you might miss the point.

When you start doing ORIENTATION on your own, here are some of the questions you can ask to get your ORIENTATION right.

- Which book of the Bible am I reading?
- Where is that book in the Bible?
- What difference does that make?
- What do I know about the book of the Bible I am reading from?
- What type of writing is it (a letter, a book about historical events, a book about God's Word to His people through prophets, poetry...)?
- Who wrote it and why? Who were the first readers of the book and what was their situation?
- Where have I got to so far in the book?

The starting point for getting to grips with ORIENTATION is just having these questions in mind, seeing that they are important to understanding what you are reading and having a go at them. You don't have to know all the answers to these questions for every book of the Bible. Just have the questions and be willing to find out the answers.

In Appendix 3 you will find a time line which can help answer some of the questions above. Hopefully the worked through examples throughout the book will give you some ideas too.

Choose Bible reading notes that include some ORIENTATION, ask someone to help you with ORIENTATION as you start a new book of the Bible, but most of all just read carefully and look for the clues in the Bible itself. If you start asking the right questions now you will start building up a growing picture of the Bible and you'll get into a great habit that will help you whenever you open up the Bible in whatever situation.

A good general pattern for your Bible reading then is to work through whole books. Consider starting with one of the books about Jesus' life, death, resurrection and ascension. Mark's gospel is often recommended for first timers. Then you could read a book of the Old Testament–it does make sense to start with Genesis. Next you might want to read about what happened after Jesus went back to heaven and how the first churches got started in Acts. Try one of the letters Paul wrote to various churches. Then get back into the Old Testament for a bit. We're back to that idea of a balanced diet. It isn't a question of reading the whole Bible in the shortest amount of time, but we should be aiming to read the whole counsel of God as we have our quiet times over the years. Remember that although the Bible is broken up into books it is one book with one big story line. We will be able to dig deeper and deeper into what God is saying to us as we build up an understanding of the whole of God's Word.

Good Bible reading notes will take you through a variety of books of the Bible in chunks that you can handle. After a stint in a book of the Old Testament (generally longer than New Testament books) they might take you to a short letter by Paul before returning to finish off or do another section of the Old Testament book you were reading.

Back to our quiet time. Your Bible is in its usual place. You've even left a bookmark in it to show you where you got to last time. You've asked for God's help, you've done a bit of ORIENTATION and read your chosen passage for the day.

If you're using Bible reading notes they might well ask you some questions about what you have read, get you thinking about how they apply to your life and get you praying about it. Good questions will get you looking at what you have just read and make sure you've got the flow of what is happening or being said. They will help you draw out what it means and the difference it should make to you. Whether or not you are using notes here are some questions that you can ask of any passage after you have read it.

- What do these verses teach me about God?

- What do these verses teach me about me?
- What do I need to change?
- How do I need to pray?
- What questions do I still have and who could I ask for help?

Have you ever heard the expression 'like water off a duck's back'? If you've ever seen water run off a duck's back you'll know what it means. The water doesn't get absorbed at all, nothing sinks in, it just runs straight off leaving the duck dry. This is obviously very useful if you are a duck, *But this is not what our Bible reading should be like!* God's Word should not just be soaking us to our skin, but getting right under it.

So how can we minimise the foam and fill up our quiet times to the brim? We want to face the difficulties head on and get rid of the distractions. Let's summarise our helpful tips so far:

When you come to read the Bible:

- Have a plan for what you are reading—what are you tackling now and what is next?

- Have a pattern for your time in God's Word. Don't start from scratch each time you read it.

- If it is useful get Bible reading notes to help you with both the above.

- Have people to go to with the questions you have.

- And last but not least....just have a go and keep having a go! It's not a race or a test. It's the stream of water that will refresh and feed your roots. Think trees and Psalm 1, not hair!

So what's next in our quiet time? It's time to think about praying through our day. Hopefully the examples we've gone through in the chapters on prayer have given us some hints already, but let's look back at our list of froth and foam. You know the list of problems, distractions and difficulties we tend to come up against as we try and have a quiet time.

Well problems such as drawing a blank and not knowing where to start should be less of an

issue as we pray about the day ahead of us. For this part of your quiet time at least the main content should be relatively easy to access!

A drifting mind however is a regular source of foam and distraction when we pray. At least when we read the Bible we have the book there, the words are in front of us, our notes alongside perhaps. There is something to look at and work through. With praying, however, mental drift is even harder to combat.

Here are some of the 'drifty' problems we've already noted.

- You get distracted by things going on around you or by all the things whirring round in your head.

- You can't concentrate.

- You just fall asleep.

How can we combat mental drift? How can we anchor our brains in the few minutes we give to praying each day?

Look back at the plan you made. What can you tweak to minimise mental drift? For example—if you tend to fall asleep last thing at night or when you have just woken up move your quiet time to a different slot or sit on a hard seat or arm a trusted someone with a bucket of cold water!

Have you ever considered vocalising your prayers? NOT so that anyone else can hear you–that is either showing off or just embarrassing! Even just moving your lips can act as a brain anchor. D.A. Carson writes:

"the energy devoted to expressing your thoughts in words and sentences will order and discipline your mind, and help deter meandering."[1]

Having something visual to remind you what you are doing can also anchor a drifting mind.

We've seen that God's priorities for our prayers are made clear to us in the Bible. Why not keep the Bible passage you have been reading open in front of you and link your NOW thinking to something specific in your day. Write or print out the Lord's prayer and some of the other prayers from the Bible we looked at in chapter 6 and stick them into the front cover of your Bible or a notebook. Not only does this help to keep your mind from drifting, but it also combats the worry of forgetting God's priorities for your prayers.

Similar to vocalising your prayers is writing them down/typing them up. Don't think great long essays (brilliant if that's what you want to do of course!), but consider jotting down some bullet points. This forces us to take a bit of time over praying, helps us to look back and thank God, and keeps us concentrating.

[1] Don Carson *A call to Spiritual reformation*–page 21 in 1994 reprint

So get disciplined and try some anti-mental drift devices. But the real key to getting your brain anchored is to keep remembering why it is worth the effort. Remember who you are talking to and how it is possible that you can talk to Him.

On top of mental drift several other problems can bombard us as we move from praying for our day to praying more widely.

- You can't remember what or who you prayed for last time you prayed.

- You can't think who or what to pray for or you can think of five hundred things and don't know where to start!

The real issue here is deciding what/who you are going to commit to pray for over the course of the coming term/year/month.... and then organising some sort of a list so that you can regularly pray for those people and situations you have chosen.

In chapter 5 we mentioned the following possibilities:

- YOUR LOCAL CHURCH

The leaders.
Faithful preaching of God's Word.
Particular events coming up.
Your youth group.
Missionaries or Christian groups supported by your church

- THE WORLD

   Christians and Christian ministry around
   the world.

   Places of particular suffering.

- PEOPLE

   Your family.

   Christian friends.

   Friends who are not Christians.

   People known personally to you in
   difficulty.

- YOUR SCHOOL/WORKPLACE

   People you find difficult.

   Opportunities for the good news about
   Jesus to be shared.

How does that list make you feel? I feel a bit
overwhelmed just typing it up! But that is why
we need a system. Not to overburden us—but
to make a realistic commitment to praying for
certain people and situations.

Having brainstormed what you might pray
for, next work out the time you have to pray.

I have six days when my regular prayer slot
happens. I feel I should plan for seven days—
but being realistic one slot of prayers would
regularly be neglected. So that leaves six!
When I started this system I bought a plastic
wallet (helpfully divided into 6 sections) and
a pack of index cards. I then decided how
many different things I could realistically pray
for each day. For me that came out as about

five. This meant that I could plan to pray for the following each day:

- a daily prayer point for my children (I pray separately for and with my husband each day).

- an element of my local church.

- a Christian friend/family.

- a friend/family member who isn't a Christian/a regular time of meeting with non-Christians.

- and one other: it could be a person or something else that's going on in my week–like writing this book....

So when I come to pray on a Monday morning I take out my five Monday index cards. On each card is written a name or an event or a particular thing to pray for. On the back of some of the cards I might have a post-it note with three points to pray for someone which I can update when I phone them or get an e-mail.

Then I pray about each card in turn. When I have finished a card it goes to the back of the Monday pile. That way if I don't get all five cards done the neglected ones from this week will be top of the pile next week.

Comparing my list of five things above with the big list of ideas we started with you can see that I am not covering everything. At the moment for example, my personal prayer for the world is pretty rubbish. This is not the perfect system! But it does mean that early in the morning when I have a list of jobs clamouring for attention in my fuzzy mind I do pray in a relatively concentrated manner most days. And if I miss a day (to be honest I should say *"When"* I miss a day)–I normally miss a different day the next week and so people eventually get prayed for.

Your system will be different–maybe screen based not index cards for example. Your list will be different–shorter/longer/no children/lots of brothers and sisters.....Our systems will almost definitely change–to allow for changes in our lifestyle, our circle of friends, what we spend our time doing ....And as we learn more about God's desires for our prayers from His Word.

Don't worry if you just have one thing to pray for each day. Much better to plan something straightforward you can manage than to develop an over-ambitious, over complicated system that needs a 500 page booklet to explain it. Try one a day for a month and then consider adding in another point after that.

I want to end this chapter by thinking about a final pair of trouble makers: fear and faffing. The thing that makes these two so dangerous is that they can creep into quiet time because you are trying to follow the very hints and tips we have been exploring. Don't get me wrong—it is brilliant to plan carefully, to put some of the above ideas into practice– but only because they can help us with what we are trying to do.

Imagine someone is preparing to climb a mountain. They can't just set off in a t-shirt, shorts and flip-flops and hope for the best. It is important that they are well equipped or they won't get far before they either have to turn back, or worse–get into difficulty.

However, imagine someone has gone into a mountaineering shop and bought up every gadget and bit of equipment they sell.

- 5 different pairs of boots for different conditions.

- 6 thicknesses of sleeping bag just in case.

- A 4 ring gas burner.

- A camping table for a family of 5.

- An army knife with 60 attachments.

This so called 'equipment' is going to make it very hard for them to get anywhere. They are so fearful of not having the right stuff that they are not going to make any progress at all.

We can pack pretty lightly for this expedition into quiet times. Pack a Bible, and perhaps some Bible reading notes. Have a reminder of God's desires for our prayers and some kind of list of who/what you want to pray for.

But whatever you do don't forget to pack Grace! Without it the expedition is doomed. With all this talk of lists and systems, planning and practical skills, don't fall into the trap of thinking this is something you have to do a certain way to get it right. Jesus has got it right for us! The only right that matters is the right we have to be God's children because of the work of the Lord Jesus—John 1:12. If you are

a Christian you have been given right-ness with God. We are not setting off to try and impress God. We are already there because of what Jesus has done for us! Quiet times are just a great and important part of being there. Of being part of God's family...Righteous, Forgiven, Saved by Grace.

All the hints and the tips in the world are only helpful if they free us up to get to know God better. If they burden us with a wrong idea of what we need to do to please God then they are worse than all the problems, difficulties and distractions we are trying to get rid of.

At the end of the day (or whenever you have planned to do it!) just gracefully tilt your glass and pour. In other words: don't stress—just have a quiet time and enjoy some dedicated time with God.

WHO'S AFRAID OF THE BIG BAD BREATH?

Exposing some of the choices

we face and make daily

Can you remember right back in the hazy mists of time to when you started this book? It all began with an Introduction. Just in case you haven't fondly memorised the whole book I'll remind you how it began.

"Texts, Twitter, Facebook, the world wide web on your mobile phone—we can keep in touch with everyone all the time. We can find out about anything anywhere...."

But what do I know about what goes into your brain and emotions and how it gets there? I know the things that I welcome into my brain and my emotions each day. I also know the things I try my best to shut out. But what about you? Who or what do you choose to listen to regularly? Don't just think face to face conversations. What do you read, watch, listen to, see, dwell on and daydream about? Think about all the pages, screens, headphones, billboards and adverts as well as all the actual people you have contact with.

Take today or yesterday – could you list all the input you received?

If I can take you back to the Introduction one more time – this time to the end. I asked you the following question:

> "The floodgates are open for the messages from the world to stream into our lives – do you even open the door a centimetre to let what God has to say in? Isn't it time you did? Read on!"

Well you've done it. You've read on and on and on. Don't worry, I'll shut up soon I promise! We've covered lots of 'whys' and 'hows' and 'what ifs'. We've established the idea of a point in your day given over to God's Word and talking to Him. It's my prayer that with God's help you'll feel eager and able to make that point a regular feature of your day to day life.

That you'll open the door wide to what God has to say.

But what about the floodgates – all the other inputs that fill our hearts and minds? Just because we have a quiet time doesn't mean that everything else falls silent. Think again about the input you've received recently.

Here are some of mine from the last forty-eight hours: radio, children's TV, various other TV programmes, the latest James Bond film, texts from Christian and non-Christian friends, e-mails and adverts (online, through the post, on TV), people's Facebook comments, Christian music, conversations with Christian friends and family, the Bible, preaching at church half listened to while looking after my three year old, a conversation at the school gate with my son's teacher, mealtime conversation with my family...and so on.

So what do you think of what I am inputting into my life? More to the point—what do you think God thinks? Are there any inputs that shouldn't be there at all? What is missing? Is every input either pleasing or displeasing to God? Permitted or forbidden? If so how do we know which is which? And what about the inputs that I have no control over, the decisions my parents or teachers make? What do I do with those?

I want to take a look at how we might start to answer some of these questions, to give us some tools to help us take a good and challenging look at what we let into our hearts day by day. There are no prizes for figuring out what our main tools are going to be in this task! Yes–it's prayer and Bible study.

We are going to focus here on how the Bible can help us in this area, but let me encourage you to pray about it. Stop now and think through your list of inputs. Thank God for the inputs in your life that are growing your faith in Him. Say sorry to God for any inputs that you know are not pleasing to Him. Ask God to help you spot any situations or friendships you need to back out of, music or TV shows to switch off, an ungodly Facebook persona to put an end to…or whatever it is you are not sure about. Ask God to help you now as you read on and build up a clearer idea of how to look into all this.

Before we go any further I want to get something straight. The Bible is very clear that it isn't the things we touch or eat (in other words external inputs) that are the real problem. The problem is our heart.

Listen to Jesus teaching the Pharisees in Mark chapter 7. PAUSE!

ORIENTATION MARK

We're in the gospel of Mark—one of the four books at the start of the New Testament that tell us about Jesus' life, death and resurrection. Jesus is talking to the Pharisees—the religious leaders of the day. They are opposed to Jesus and have just challenged Him about not observing a particular religious rule involving a special type of washing. Jesus switches the focus from the external to the internal.

PLAY: MARK 7:20-23

[20]He (Jesus) went on: "What comes out of a person is what defiles them. [21]For it is from within, out of a person's heart, that evil thoughts come—sexual immorality, theft, murder, [22]adultery, greed, malice, deceit, lewdness, envy, slander, arrogance and folly. [23]All these evils come from inside and defile a person."

The bottom line is that even if we put ourselves into total isolation we would still sin. As Christians we don't make ourselves pure by excluding certain things from our lives or including others. Jesus identified the problem as our hearts and He dealt with the problem of our hearts. (You know where to look if you want to know more—Safety Note Number 1!)

After all an input is just that—something from the outside being put in. The problem is that—until Jesus returns and makes us new—every input will always be met and welcomed in by a heart that is prone to sin. We need to guard our hearts from the wrong kinds of inputs.

Later on in Mark Jesus urges His followers to take drastic steps to get rid of whatever causes them to sin (Mark 9:43-48). He teaches them to pray: lead us not into temptation.

In his letter to the Philippians Paul exhorts his fellow Christians to input only what is wholesome to their hearts.

PLAY: PHILIPPIANS 4:8.

"Whatever is true, whatever is noble, whatever is right, whatever is pure, whatever is lovely, whatever is admirable—if anything is excellent or praiseworthy—think about such things."

How much of what you and I input could be described that way? Have you ever taken the inputs you receive and held them up next to God's word and seen how they all measure up? So how do we do that? Is it possible to plot our inputs on a graph or scale or something? Well let's have a go. Try and put your inputs into the scale on the opposite page.

JO'S INPUT-OMETER

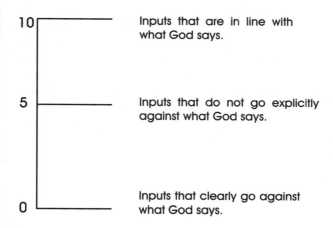

10 — Inputs that are in line with what God says.

5 — Inputs that do not go explicitly against what God says.

0 — Inputs that clearly go against what God says.

Am I really serious? Well sort of. To be honest it doesn't always work out as black and white as the diagram suggests. As I've attempted to put anything on this scale I've been saying to myself: "well that depends on..." or "but it could be...." or "not necessarily..."

Thankfully the purpose of this chapter is not to neatly box up and label our inputs–but rather to get them out in the open and take a good look. To unravel and expose the nature of what gets dumped into our hearts and minds every day and to shine God's word on it.

Go back to your list of inputs. Can you spot any that are clearly in line with what God says? From mine I might put my own quiet time. It got me looking at God's word and helped me to understand and think about what

God was saying. What about anything that is obviously out of line with what God says in His word? For me there were definitely scenes in the James Bond film that showed a life style completely against God's Word. I guess in the middle of the scale I could put the children's TV I watched with my kids. It didn't input any truths about God into our lives, but neither did it directly promote anything against God. Are there inputs like that for you?

Have a go:

How in line is this input with God's word?

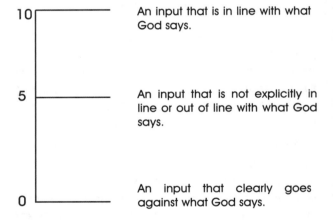

10 — An input that is in line with what God says.

5 — An input that is not explicitly in line or out of line with what God says.

0 — An input that clearly goes against what God says.

Here are a couple of examples of inputs around a particular subject and how they might match up to God's word.

Let's take the area of money first. We might have something that looks like this:

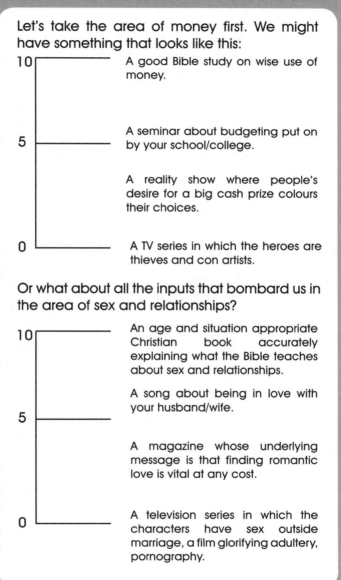

10 — A good Bible study on wise use of money.

5 — A seminar about budgeting put on by your school/college.

A reality show where people's desire for a big cash prize colours their choices.

0 — A TV series in which the heroes are thieves and con artists.

Or what about all the inputs that bombard us in the area of sex and relationships?

10 — An age and situation appropriate Christian book accurately explaining what the Bible teaches about sex and relationships.

A song about being in love with your husband/wife.

5 —

A magazine whose underlying message is that finding romantic love is vital at any cost.

0 — A television series in which the characters have sex outside marriage, a film glorifying adultery, pornography.

Remember: this is not a set of discrete and precise categories. A few things are clearly either at the top or the bottom of the scale, but mostly there are lots of ifs and buts. Not much gets close to being neutral when you really look at it. A song about love within a marriage is not explicitly against God. God designed marriage and wants husbands and wives to love each other! But the song may be sending all sorts of messages about marriage that are far from in line with what God says: you can do anything if you have someone who loves you; you don't need God if you have a husband; marriage goes on for eternity; marriage is only worth the effort if you feel like singing a love song.... Should the singer's real life marriage have anything to do with how we listen to their song? I've put a seminar on budgeting in the middle of the scale—but how comfortably can it sit there? While it probably won't encourage theft or dishonesty it probably won't take into consideration the Bible's commands to be generous with our money.

Even the top of the scale isn't always clear cut. Just because something is explicitly in line with God's commands doesn't make it the right input for us. For example, a Biblically true book about sex which would be great for a married couple to read will not contain wise input for a thirteen year old. It will cover things that aren't good for him/her to think about—and also miss out a lot he/she needs to consider.

And don't even get me started about how complicated it gets at the other end of the scale. Does a film have to be totally about something that displeases God to score a zero– or just have one bad element in the storyline? Am I saying we just shouldn't watch or read anything that contains anything that goes against God? Is it OK if the ungodly behaviour in the story line is punished–like in a detective series when the murderer gets caught? What about the fact that lots of the laughs, beauty, and general entertainment in the show/book/ film are about good things like friendship, stunning scenery, family life, loyalty....

And at the end of the day surely it is OK to just chill out and not have to think for a bit?

Well–what do you reckon? How would you answer these questions from what we have read so far in this book? How would the writer of Psalm 1 or the apostle Paul answer them?

Annoyingly for the purposes of this book I am more interested in raising the questions at this stage than answering them.

I'm not going to tell you what you can and can't do. I'm not going to give you a list of the films you are not allowed to watch and the music you can't listen to. For one thing it would be out of date before this book gets to press, let alone before you read it. More importantly the Bible doesn't give me a list to pass on to you.

However, the Bible does give us some guidelines here, some do's and don'ts that can help us navigate tricky territory. Just so you know—the statements I've given you below are not direct quotes from the Bible—they often summarise teaching that runs throughout God's Word. The Bible references are a sample so you can check that what I've summarised does indeed come from God and not me. Don't forget to consider the ORIENTATION as you go look things up!

COMMAND FROM GOD	EXAMPLE OF OBEDIENCE
Don't lie. Obey the law. Exodus 20:16; Ephesians 4:25; Romans 13:1.	Don't go to an 18 film if you are 13 or even 17 and 11 months.
Honour your parents. Exodus 20:16; Ephesians 6:1.	Don't watch or listen to something that they have told you not to.
Don't arouse sexual feelings with anyone other than your wife/husband. Genesis 2:24-25; 1 Thessalonians 4:3-7; 1 Corinthians 6:18; Ephesians 5:3.	Avoid pornography and any music, TV, films, etc. that are unhelpful in this area.
Don't make it hard for people to obey Jesus. Help other Christians to obey. 1 Corinthians 8:12; Mark 9:42, Hebrews 10:24.	Don't do anything that causes someone else to sin even if you are fine with it/old enough/your parents say it is OK.
Think about what is true, noble, right, pure, lovely, admirable, excellent and praiseworthy. Philippians 4:8.	Get rid of whatever turns your thoughts away from these things.
Don't be greedy, be content, don't covet (long for) what other people have. Exodus 20:17; Philippians 4:11-13; Colossians 3:6.	Don't pour over magazines or adverts if you know they are going to make you desperate for things you haven't got.
Speak in a wholesome, helpful and thankful way. Don't be obscene or coarse in the way you speak. Ephesians 4:29; 5:4.	Think honestly about how various inputs effect the way you speak.
Do everything to the glory of God, in Jesus' name giving thanks to God. 1 Corinthians 10:31; Colossians 3:17.	Ask yourself can you do this and represent Jesus? Will this action help others to see how amazing God is and to obey Him?

Well that's certainly shone some light onto the situation. It's a bit like lifting a rock and watching the creepy crawlies scatter in every direction. How is the list of what you input into your life liking the spotlight?

Notice I say 'the things *you* input into your life'. But of course it's not always our choice is it.

Whereas things like:

- the music you listen to in private.
- what you watch when you have control of the remote.
- what you read when you're on your own.
- what you let your mind wander to when you daydream.
- what you bring up in conversation. what you look up on the Internet.
- whether you stay or leave in certain situations.

These are up to you:

Inputs that come at us in a group situation or when we are out and about may be out of our control.

Conversations, music choices, magazine articles, billboards, Internet sites, TV programmes etc....... chosen by others, but right there in your face.

The options open to you in these situations will vary hugely–how much you can influence a group choice, your opportunities to do something different or leave... The one thing that is always under your control, however, is how you react. How much attention you pay something at the time and how you think about it afterwards. Who you chat to about it and how you chat about it. Whether you dare to look at it under the bright light of God's word or hide it away as a separate part of your life.

Just pause for a minute. Where would you put yourself on the scale below?

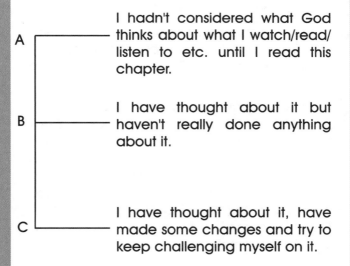

A — I hadn't considered what God thinks about what I watch/read/ listen to etc. until I read this chapter.

B — I have thought about it but haven't really done anything about it.

C — I have thought about it, have made some changes and try to keep challenging myself on it.

If this is all new please don't feel overwhelmed. To just start thinking in this way and to ask God to help you is great. This is a life-long task. New inputs are constantly arriving and as we read the Bible and are taught and encouraged by other Christians old inputs may need to be re-evaluated.

Just have a go. Start by praying and then think of two actions you could take as a result of this chapter. Is there an input that is completely within your control that you just need to get rid of? Are there predictable situations where you know you just need to walk away or change the subject? Could you plan to take some time at the end of the day/week to take a closer look at some seemingly neutral inputs and expose them to God's Word?

Perhaps you need to just resolve to keep this kind of thinking more present in your day to day life. Pray for God's help now you've chosen your action points.

So what's all this about bad breath? We found out in chapter 4 that the Bible is God-breathed and we briefly asked ourselves who or what the majority of our input was breathed out by. Whose exhaled air are we greedily gulping in? In this chapter we have been submitting those inputs to the authority of God's breathed out words and checking how sweetly they smell.

So if the breath stinks hold your nose, and when it's God-breathed take deep breaths. How full is your life of God-breathed inputs? Put some more in–freshen the breath in your life!

I must warn you that most of what you unearth as you evaluate your inputs will be things you need to think carefully about, that don't have an easy 'yes' or 'no' answer. Older Christians may give you conflicting answers. You might feel confident about a decision at first, but after a few months begin to feel torn again. What you need for this ongoing process is *Wisdom*. I'm not talking about being clever– if you were thinking of an owl wearing glasses and looking like a professor–well don't! When

the Bible speaks of wisdom, it means being ready to put God in charge. To be foolish is not to do badly in an exam, but to say there is no God. Admitting there is a God and submitting to Him–that is wisdom[1]. If you honestly and willingly lay the inputs of your life open on the table for God to see and ask Him to help you make wise choices–He will.

---

[1] See Psalm 14:1; Proverbs 1:7

As we've found out–when we come to do this there are no short cuts. There's no gadget we can buy—no spiritual breathalyser that will do all the work for us![2] That's why I have raised more questions than I have answered. The good news is that the real issue here is not our *accuracy* at weighing things up and sticking them on a scale, but our *readiness* to open things up to God's authority.

Well helpfully we are back to the whole point of the book: grace-fully keep reading God's Word and pray! The more we talk to God about things and the more we let Him talk to us in His Word–the better equipped we will be to do the bad breath test on all the inputs that flood into our lives.

---

[2]The best I can do on that front is: if in doubt don't touch it with a barge pole!

WITH OR WITHOUT?

The difference 10 minutes make

I ONCE watched a film which explored how someone's life could go in a completely different direction all because they missed a train. A two minute difference set up two very different storylines. In the first scenario a woman just manages to catch a train, arrives home quickly and uncovers a secret that changes everything. The alternative storyline sees her get home thirty minutes later. The secret remains a secret and her life follows a very different path.

A few minutes can make a big difference.

Let's try and tease out the difference 10 minutes[1] spent in a quiet time could make to someone's day and–eventually–their life.

I say 'tease out' because having a quiet time isn't a magic formula. It isn't a case of read this passage and then this will or won't happen. It isn't the case that when you miss

---

[1] A random number I have pretty much picked out of the air–up to you how long you spend

your quiet time your day will go dreadfully or that when you have a quiet time all will go smoothly and well.

This is not a scientific experiment! We are going to somewhat clumsily stick a random quiet time into an imagined day and consider what difference it would make. Oh and by the way–I say we, but really I mean you!

At the opticians they might ask you: "With or without?" i.e. "Is your sight better with this lens or without it?" What about 24 hours of your life? Better with or without a quiet time? Let's imagine a day without a quiet time first.

- *It's breakfast time and your brother/sister is annoying you. Do you:*

a. snap at him/her.

b. complain to your parents.

c. grin and bear it while plotting revenge.

d. ask him/her about their day.

e. other: _____

and in doing that do you:

1. Please God in your reaction, and help others see what He is like.

2. Displease God and dishonour His name.

- *A friend at school asks you how your weekend was. Do you:*

a. make up something really interesting.

b. mutter something and ask them about theirs.

c. tell them about the telly you watched.

d. try and tell them something about what you learned at church.

e. other: _____

and in doing that do you:

1. Please God in your reaction, and help others see what He is like.

2. Displease God and dishonour His name.

• *It's break time at school and your friends are all looking at a magazine. It's one your Mum isn't keen on you reading. Do you:*

a. go for it anyway.

b. promise yourself you'll stop if something dodgy comes up.

c. pretend to be involved but think about something else entirely.

d. walk away.

e. other _____.

and in doing that do you:

1. Please God in your reaction, and help others see what He is like.

2. Displease God and dishonour His name.

• *You're walking home with a friend who has been coming to youth group lately. They ask you a question about last week's Bible passage. You're not sure who else can hear you! Do you:*

a. pretend you didn't hear and change the subject.

b. tell them you have no idea in a disinterested way.

c. have a go at answering the question.

d. admit you don't know, but promise to look into it.

e. other _____.

and in doing that do you:

1. Please God in your reaction, and help others see what He is like.

2. Displease God and dishonour His name.

I'm trusting you answered honestly. No one is going to check of course—but the exercise isn't going to work if you just answered the way you think you should have. Imagine how wrong someone's glasses would be if they pretended to see better than they really could!

Now this isn't a scientific experiment. Of course it is possible to go through a day doing lots of the 'right' things without having a quiet time, or to have a quiet time and go really wrong all day. What matters is what is going on in our hearts. We might do the right thing but for the wrong reason or we might do the right thing because God goes on helping us whether we have had a quiet time or not. A multiple choice test can't give us a picture of our heart relationship with God. But it can nudge our thinking in the right direction.

So keeping this in mind let's move on to our imaginary day with a quiet time:

- *It's Monday morning. You're having a quiet time. You have already prayed for God's help and then read Psalm 1.*

Remember the Wow prayer in chapter 6? After reading this you might pray something along the lines of:

Wow: Dear Father God, you give Your people your wonderful law and you watch over their ways.

Ow: I'm sorry that I so often listen to what sinners have to say and ignore your Word. Like the other day when.........Please forgive me because Jesus died for me.

Now: Thank You that I've made time today to read the Bible and pray–help me to do this tomorrow. Help me to turn to your Word more regularly. Help me to know what to do in break time today when the others are reading that magazine. In Jesus' name, Amen.

You move from praying about Psalm 1 to talking to God about your day. This is what comes to mind:

1. My brother/sister is so annoying at the moment. He/she is so full of energy in the morning and I just want to eat my breakfast in silence.

2. Lunch time–everyone will pour over *The Magazine*. If I don't join in they'll think I'm weird, but Psalm 1 talks about following God's Word and not pouring over stuff that is against what He says.

3. I wonder if I'll manage to tell people anything about youth group when they ask me how my weekend was?

As well as your Bible reading and prayer for your day you have planned to pray for a different friend or family member each day of the week.

• *On a Monday you pray for your friend _____. You're not sure if he/she is a Christian but they have been coming to church with you most weeks. You're aware that they are very quiet about it at school though and tend to go along with the crowd.*

Does thinking about your day like this make life feel like one big battle? Well, if you're a Christian then getting out of bed in the morning is pretty much like going out to war! While having a quiet time is not a lucky charm that will make everything go smoothly for you– it is a chance to gather the right equipment for the specific battles ahead and to have thought strategically about what you're about to face. Back to our questions:

• *You've read Psalm 1 and prayed, but now it's breakfast time and your brother/sister is annoying you. Do you:*

    a. snap at him/her.

    b. complain to your parents.

    c. grin and bear it while plotting revenge.

    d. ask him/her about their day.

    e. other: _____

and in doing that do you:

1. Please God in your reaction, and help others see what He is like.
2. Displease God and dishonour His name.

• *A friend at school asks you how your weekend was. Do you:*

a. make up something really interesting.

b. mutter something and ask them about theirs.

c. tell them about the telly you watched.

d. try and tell them something about what your learned at church.

e. other: _____

and in doing that do you:

1. Please God in your reaction, and help others see what He is like.
2. Displease God and dishonour His name.

• *At school your friends are all looking at a magazine. It's one your Mum isn't keen on you reading. Do you:*

a. go for it anyway.

b. promise yourself you'll stop if something dodgy comes up.

c. pretend to be involved but think about something else entirely.

d. walk away.

e. other _____.

and in doing that do you:

1. Please God in your reaction, and help others see what He is like.
2. Displease God and dishonour His name.
• *You're walking home with a friend who has been coming to youth group lately. They ask you a question. You're not sure who else can hear you! Do you:*
a. pretend you didn't hear and change the subject.
b. tell them you have no idea in a disinterested way.
c. have a go at answering the question.
d. admit you don't know, but promise to look into it.
e. other _____.

and in doing that do you:

1. Please God in your reaction, and help others see what He is like.
2. Displease God and dishonour His name.

Any different? Would reading Psalm 1 and asking God to use it in your life change anything? Would asking God to help you please Him? Would it really make a difference? Did you get any sense of whether time spent on your own with God could touch the rest of your day?

I'm not imagining that we would suddenly react in a God-pleasing way at every turn. I'm not saying that your brother would no longer annoy you. Neither am I saying that we would be super bold in telling everyone about Jesus. It isn't a magic trick. We don't wave our wand–have a quiet time, say abracadabra, and hey presto we're perfect.

But if what we have said about God is true, what we have said about His Word, and the access we have to Him in prayer–then it has to make a difference. So why is that? Well I'm not claiming I can reel off the definitive answer to that question, but take a look at the following for starters:

1. God hears our prayers and answers them wisely and powerfully.
2. God's Word teaches, corrects, rebukes and trains.
3. God's Holy Spirit changes God's people through prayer and the Bible.
4. God wants us to love Him more and more.
5. God wants us to enjoy Him and enjoy obeying Him.
6. God wants people to find out how amazing He is and He wants to use us!

God is the reason that a quiet time with Him makes a difference in our lives. So what's better: with or without? I say with! And the great thing is you don't start from scratch every day. Imagine the difference a life time habit of quiet times make to our 'Imaginary Monday'

- Firstly you would be better equipped to understand and apply God's Word. In this particular situation you would be able to understand and apply Psalm 1.

- Secondly you would have an ever growing general pool of Bible knowledge to draw from as you thought through and prayed about your day. Think of an army with a bigger arsenal and more ammunition. It's just better! The more we read the Bible and the more familiar we become with it; the more Bible passages we'll have at our fingertips to teach, correct, rebuke and train us.

So for our fake Monday morning (or any day of the week for that matter!) we could add in the following passages from the Bible to inform our prayers and decisions through the day.

PAUSE! Let's not dive into unfamiliar waters without getting our bearings first. In fact it's *always* necessary to PAUSE for ORIENTATION however familiar the verses. The ORIENTATION might come more quickly to mind, but it is no less important to our understanding.

ORIENTATION

All the following passages are from the New Testament and are written after Jesus has gone back to heaven. They are all parts of letters from Paul to groups of Christians in various situations, except 1 Peter which is written by Peter–the Peter who was one of Jesus' disciples–to Christians scattered around the area and having a hard time!

PLAY: PHILIPPIANS 2:3-4

³Do nothing out of selfish ambition or vain conceit. Rather, in humility value others above yourselves, ⁴not looking to your own interests but each of you to the interests of the others.

PLAY: COLOSSIANS 3:12-14

¹²Therefore, as God's chosen people, holy and dearly loved, clothe yourselves with compassion, kindness, humility, gentleness and patience. ¹³Bear with each other and forgive one another if any of you has a grievance against someone. Forgive as the Lord forgave you. ¹⁴And over all these virtues put on love, which binds them all together in perfect unity.

PLAY: GALATIANS 5:22-23

²²But the fruit of the Spirit is love, joy, peace, forbearance, kindness, goodness, faithfulness, ²³gentleness and self-control. Against such things there is no law.

PLAY: EPHESIANS 6:1

⁶Children, obey your parents in the Lord, for this is right.

PLAY: COLOSSIANS 3:9

⁹Do not lie to each other, since you have taken off your old self with its practices.

PLAY: EPHESIANS 5:15-17

¹⁵Be very careful, then, how you live—not as unwise but as wise, ¹⁶making the most of every opportunity, because the days are evil. ¹⁷Therefore do not be foolish, but understand what the Lord's will is.

PLAY: 1 PETER 3:15

¹⁵But in your hearts revere Christ as Lord. Always be prepared to give an answer to everyone who asks you to give the reason for the hope that you have. But do this with gentleness and respect.

PLAY: COLOSSIANS 3:17

¹⁷And whatever you do, whether in word or deed, do it all in the name of the Lord Jesus, giving thanks to God the Father through Him.

As I read through those verses I'm reminded of that tree from Psalm 1. If our roots are watered regularly with passages like these imagine the difference it would make. And I'm not just talking about some imaginary scenarios—I'm talking about the real lives you and I lead day by day.

*Warning! T*ry not to think about this as simply knowing more—like revising for an exam, or praying more—like putting enough coins into a slot machine. A long-term habit of Bible reading and prayer isn't a formula—it is part of building our *relationship with God*.

Through His Word and through prayer we will get to know Him better and love Him more. We will increasingly know His heart for people and situations and we'll reflect that in our prayers. We will trust Him as we pray and we'll feel safe praying again tomorrow when it has all gone wrong. We will have more chances to say sorry, and more chances to enjoy His forgiveness. We will get grace more clearly and be less likely to forget it.

That's the biggest difference quiet times should make to our lives—*Grace*. Remember grace? Remember all the wonderful underserved gifts that God gives us: His Son, salvation, forgiveness, eternal Life... the list goes on. And it is God's word that shows it all to us—that makes us wise for salvation.

When we read the Bible, when we pray for forgiveness confident in what Jesus has done, when we spot the way God has been answering our prayers we are daily letting God remind us about grace.

We don't have quiet times so that we can gradually live a better life in order to eventually please God enough.

We can only have a quiet time because Jesus has done everything to please God for us. We can only pray because Jesus died, rose again and ascended to heaven and sits at God's right hand praying for us.

We can only benefit from God's Word because we have Jesus' Spirit in us helping us to understand, to remember, to obey.

We can only keep going when we fail again and again to have a quiet time because Jesus has made it possible for us to be God's accepted, and beloved children.

It is because of Jesus that we can always come to our Father for forgiveness and help.

Remember: a sorted relationship with God is a free gift. A quiet time helps us enjoy that gift and experience it more fully everyday. It helps us to continue in God's kindness.

Never mind the optician's lenses—I want to know what sort of day you hunger for. Is it one with or without a quiet time; with or without talking to and hearing from your Father God?

IN CONCLUSION

Ladies and gentlemen we will

soon be beginning our descent

AT THE start of the book we considered the importance of the safety announcements before we took off on a flight. Well if reading this book has been a flight then we're just about to start the descent. We're about to land and the journey is nearly finished. I do hope you have had a good flight!

One final job before we come down to earth with a bump: let's take a mental picture of the view from the air. Take a look at the questions below to help you focus on the big picture of the Christian life.

• What would you say is the end goal of being a Christian?

• What is great about following Jesus?

• Why choose to have Jesus as your King?

Did you know that God made us to see and point out and enjoy His greatness? Sin spoils this though. It cuts us off from the God we were made to enjoy and serve. With sin in the picture, His relationship with us must be as our judge.

But God spoilt the power of sin! Jesus died and rose again just as He said He would. By those historical acts He gives us confidence in His authority and the truth of what He says. He gives us confidence that we are forgiven, that we are God's friends, His children. He gives us His Spirit to make us more like Him and to show us that we can come confidently to God no matter that we've done. He gives us grace.

The goal of being a Christian is to just go on and on receiving this grace from Him. We are simply to have a go at life each day as God's child under His care and protection; to wait faithfully until we are with Him face to face in His perfect Kingdom where we will enjoy Him perfectly and eternally.

Wow—what a view! Remember it! Remember the big picture of God's grace. It is this view that will help you to open up your Bible reading notes again when you find them under your bed covered in dust. It is this view that will keep you going when you've started and given up on three different prayer lists.

And what about when you finally do manage something and you're not sure you even got it 'right' as it doesn't seem to make much difference? What will help you then?

Exactly! Remember and never forget the massive picture of God's *Grace*.

Now for the landing.... finally.... Before we took off I strongly encouraged you to read some Safety Notes. Now we have landed please don't ditch them. They are even more necessary on the ground than when reading this book. Up in the air I've had lots of chances to chuck in extra Safety Notes to make this a GRACE-full flight. Now we've landed it's not up to me any more. It's up to you.

Or is it? Who is going to keep you going?

Only God can do that! So does that let you off the hook? No way.

Paul writes this in his letter to the Christians in a place called Philippi.

PLAY: PHILIPPIANS 2:12,13

"...continue to work out your salvation with fear and trembling, for it is God who works in you, to will and to act according to His good purpose."

So go for it–in His strength. Let's finish this book with a prayer.

Dear Father God,

Thank you for giving me the opportunity to write this book and for giving _____ the chance to read it. We need You to work in us to help us treat Jesus as the amazing King He is, and to make us more like Jesus.

Your Word teaches us that reading Your Word and praying is an important and amazing part of that. Please help us to persevere in making time for a quiet time. Help us to honestly find the best time and place for that in the lives we are living right now.

Most of all please may we understand more and more what Jesus has done for all those who follow Him. Protect us from thinking we can do anything to earn a right status before Him. Keep us from thinking that we can do anything to spoil the saving work He has done for all those who put their trust in Him.

We ask all this confidently because Jesus died and rose again and right now sits at your right hand praying for His people.

Amen

AUTHOR'S NOTE

In which I confess all....

IT HAS taken me about two years to write this book—on and off. That is at least 730 days! Have I had a quiet time on each and every one of those 730 days? No. Some days I have managed to pray, but not read the Bible, or I might have read the Bible but got distracted before I prayed. I have squeezed my quiet time into bits of time not useful for anything else and on several occasions have just gone without. There have been whole days when I haven't read God's word, I haven't praised Him, said sorry, thanked Him, or asked Him for help for myself and others. I have often failed to read the Bible with my three young children, or pray with them—sometimes because I have been writing this book!

My first reaction is to kick myself. To shout at myself: "You idiot! Try harder, sort it out!"

But my next reaction is to send myself back to Safety Note Number 1 and to remember God's grace.

God's grace is big enough to cover my sloppy quiet times! Thanks to Jesus I'm completely forgiven. He hasn't given up on me and left me struggling along on my own. No—He's helped me get back into His amazing Word and let me come confidently into His throne room in prayer again and again no matter what.

Do you want to know this God of grace better, to dive deeper into a grace-full life? Well – we know a good place to swim don't we! By God's grace let's read the Bible and pray!

[1]'God is a Holy God' by Paul Sheely from the CD 'The King, the snake and the promise' © 1998 Plainsong Music

APPENDIX 1–FURTHER READING

The following books are suggestions for further reading. Some are more advanced than others. If you feel you're ready for a book that will take you deeper take a look at those with a plus sign beside them.

If you feel you want to cover the basics first then go for one of the other books, maybe even the ones with a star sign beside them.

DO YOU WANT TO FIND OUT MORE ABOUT...

1. JESUS CHRIST AND WHAT HE HAS DONE

* Super Son by Andy Robb

Jesus Rose From the Dead: The Evidence by Catherine Mackenzie

*The Jesus Files by Carine Mackenzie

A Young Person's Guide to Knowing God by Patricia St. John

2. WHAT A CHRISTIAN IS

Genuine, Becoming a real teenager by C B Martin

True, Being true to yourself, your God, your relationships by Sarah Bradley

Love is: Loving Others God's Way by Laura Martin

Commanded: Your Mission–Loving Others God's Way by L H Martin

*Talk Sense by Sammy Horner

*Following God by Carine Mackenzie

Keep on Going: Youth Group Sessions on 1 Thessalonians by Nick Margesson

Get Moving: Motivation for Living by Paul White

2. WHAT THE BIBLE SAYS

The Action Bible: God's Redemptive Story by Sergio Cariello

Little Black Book: The Bible by Scott Petty

*100 Fascinating Bible Facts by Irene Howat

+ Bible Answers: Questions about the Christian Faith and Life by Derek Prime

+ Bible Overview by Steve Levy and Paul Blackham

What the Bible Means to me—Testimonies of How God's Word impacts Lives, edited by Catherine Mackenzie

66 Books One Story: A Guide to Every Book of the Bible by Paul Reynolds

3. HOW TRUSTWORTHY IS THE BIBLE?

Can We Trust What the Gospels Say About Jesus? By Andrew Errington

You Asked: Your Questions. God's Answers by William Edgar

Top 100 Questions: Remix by Richard Bewes

4. PRAYER

Massive Prayer Adventure by Sarah Mayer

Prayer is an Adventure: Building a Friendship with God by Patricia St. John

+ If God Already Knows Why Pray by Douglas Kelly

5. THE TRINITY

+ Forgotten God: Reversing Our Tragic Neglect of the Holy Spirit by Francis Chan

Little Black Book: The Holy Spirit by Scott Perry

BIBLE READING NOTES AND DEVOTIONALS:

Newness of Life: An Introduction to Daily Bible Reading by John Eddison

APPENDIX 2–THE HOLY SPIRIT

The Holy Spirit is the Third Member of the Trinity. The Trinity consists of God the Father, God the Son and God the Holy Spirit. This means that the Holy Spirit is God. The Trinity and the work of the Holy Spirit within that, need whole books of their own. I've recommended some places to look in Appendix 1. For now let me try and give you enough information to get started.

Firstly you will notice that when I talk about the Holy Spirit I use the word HE and not IT. In the Bible the Holy Spirit is referred to personally and not as an impersonal force. Christians have a personal relationship with the Holy Spirit. As you read the Bible you will see that the Holy Spirit can be grieved, sinned against and resisted. You will see that He comforts, guides and teaches God's people–changing them to become more like Jesus.

IMPORTANT NOTE: All Christians have the Holy Spirit in them—there is nothing extra that you need to do. If you are a Christian—if Jesus is your Lord and rescuer, if you are God's friend because of Jesus—then you have the Holy Spirit. No 'buts', 'ifs' or 'it depends'.....

So the Holy Spirit is God. He is personal and all Christians have been given the gift of the Holy Spirit. He lives in them. So what difference does that make? It makes all the difference in the world. It is the difference between Option 1 and Option 2 in Safety Note Number 1 way back in chapter 1. Without Him we wouldn't be Christians in the first place, let alone keep going. The Holy Spirit is with us to help and comfort us.

In the context of this book we have been reading that it is the Holy Spirit who helps us respond to the Spirit inspired Word of God. What better helper could we ask for? He wrote it! He is also our helper as we pray–every word we utter to God as Christians is uttered with the help of the Holy Spirit. We don't have to understand it or feel it or be aware of it or be able to describe it.

The Holy Spirit's help comes to us freely. Did you know that if you are a Christian the Holy Spirit has already helped you in the best way ever? He has persuaded you of the truth of the good news about Jesus. He has persuaded you of your need for rescue and that Jesus has met that need. Are you aware of His promise to keep helping you as you go on reading the Bible—He will go on persuading you that what you read is true and trustworthy. He will help you understand it and act on it and He will help you tell others about it and talk to God about it.

Thank God: Father, Son and Holy Spirit for saving you and for His promise to stay with you always.

If you are not a Christian and are longing to respond in faith to all of this–ask for the help of the Holy Spirit.

APPENDIX 3–A BIBLE OVERVIEW

We looked at the story of the Bible in one go in Chapter 1. This is what we said:

- God exists for eternity.
- God makes the world perfectly.
- People sin but God promises to solve the problem of sin.
- God relates with His people Israel: sin keeps spoiling, and God keeps promising.
- God makes particular promises about sending a rescuing King to sort out sin.
- God's people wait and wait and wait and go on sinning.
- King Jesus comes. Many refuse to believe He is the King.
- The King dies on the cross–that's the rescue!
- The King rises again and ascends to heaven.
- Jesus' friends spread the news about King Jesus.
- All sorts of people become Christians–God's new people—and start meeting together.
- Lots of letters get sent to teach the new Christians all over the place.
- Jesus returns–punishes evil and makes everything new. This is the only bit that hasn't already happened–the Bible tells us to be ready for it though!
- God exists with His people, while those who are not His people exist for eternity without Him.

Now let's try and put some of the major people and events of the Bible on a time line to help us with our ORIENTATION skills. You'll see that I have put some very rough dates next to some of the events to give an idea of the time scale involved. When BC appears after a number it means the number of years before Jesus was born and when AD appears it means the number of years after.

GENESIS

- Creation.
- Mankind disobeys God–this is often called The Fall.
- Abraham is promised: a people, a place and a blessing (2000 BC).
- Joseph and then the rest of his family go to Egypt.

EXODUS—DEUTERONOMY

- Moses and God's people–Israel—are rescued from slavery in Egypt (1450BC).
- God gives His people the Ten Commandments and many other laws about being His people in His place.
- The people grumble and mistrust God and wander in the desert for 40 years.
- The people eventually are at the edge of the land God has promised them.

JOSHUA, JUDGES AND RUTH

- Joshua leads God's people into God's promised land–you might have heard of the 'Battle of Jericho', but there were lots of cities to take!
- The people live in the land, but disobey God. God sends people called judges to rescue them and bring them back to Him. This keeps happening. The last judge is Samuel.

1 SAMUEL AND 2 SAMUEL, 1 KINGS

- The people want a King. Saul is their first king, but he disobeys God and David (think David and Goliath) becomes king of Israel (1050BC).
- God promises David that someone descended from him will be a perfect, eternal King.
- David's son is Solomon (think wisdom) and after Solomon dies the kingdom of Israel splits in two. The Northern Kingdom is called Israel, and the Southern Kingdom is called Judah. God's promises relate to Judah so watch what happens to them carefully (950BC).

1 KINGS—MALACHI

- We follow the story of both the Northern Kingdom which eventually gets wiped out and the Southern Kingdom which ends up exiled in Babylon (think Daniel in the lion's den). A big problem for Israel is that they keep worshipping false gods or idols and there are hardly any good kings at all in this time. God keeps warning them using His prophets (you might have heard of Elijah for example) but they don't listen.

- Eventually the Southern Kingdom get back to the land God gave them, but things don't look great. God has made fantastic promises to them and He has kept everyone so far. Will God's people trust Him to send the eternal rescuing King He has promised and to sort out the problem of sin? Or will they go on disobeying Him and trying things their way?

400 YEARS LATER....

MATTHEW, MARK, LUKE, JOHN

- Jesus is born.
- Jesus dies on the cross (30AD).
- Jesus rises again and ascends to heaven.

ACTS—JUDE

- Jesus sends the Holy Spirit on the 12 apostles and the good news about Jesus starts to spread.

- Saul who persecuted Christians becomes a Christian and is known as Paul.

- The good news continues to spread around the world and churches are set up. Paul and others write to the churches to teach them about Jesus. Christians face lots of opposition and persecution.

REVELATION

- John receives a vision (95AD) of what is really happening in the world from the vantage point of God's throne room. We find out a bit more about Jesus' return and the final conquering of evil.

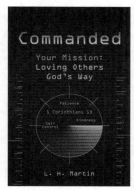

FOR THE BOYS: Everywhere around us the clock is ticking. Everyone has a mission they are trying to achieve. Some are exciting—climb mountains, cure cancer, capture criminals. Some are, well, boring—make beds, wash dishes, pull weeds. And then some are commanded. If we are Christians we have a mission written in God's Word, The Bible. It is not all about you though. It's about honouring God by the way you live. ISBN: 978-1-78191-120-4

FOR THE GIRLS.... Do you think that sometimes the whole world seems to be singing about love—yet nobody really knows what it's all about? We need to find out about the One who is love and who gave it to us in the first place. God! Based on 1 Corinthians 13 this book is a month's worth of daily readings and devotions on the theme of God's Love. ISBN: 978-1-84550-971-2

CHRISTIAN FOCUS PUBLICATIONS

Christian Focus · Christian Heritage · CF4K · Mentor

Christian Focus Publications publishes books for adults and children under its four main imprints: Christian Focus, CF4K, Mentor and Christian Heritage. Our books reflect our conviction that God's Word is reliable and Jesus is the way to know Him, and live for ever with Him.

Our children's publication list includes a Sunday School curriculum that covers pre-school to early teens, and puzzle and activity books. We also publish personal and family devotional titles, biographies and inspirational stories that children will love.

If you are looking for quality Bible teaching for children then we have an excellent range of Bible stories and age-specific theological books.

From pre-school board books to teenage apologetics, we have it covered!

Find us at our web page:
www.christianfocus.com

CF4·K
Because you're never too young to know Jesus